Nationalism

Concepts in the Social Sciences

Series Editor: Frank Parkin

Published Titles

Concepts in the Social Sciences

Nationalism

Craig Calhoun

Open University Press
Buckingham

Open University Press
Celtic Court
22 Ballmoor
Buckingham
MK18 1XW

First Published 1997

A catalogue record of this book is available from the British Library

ISBN 0 335 19301 3 (pb)   0 335 19302 1 (hb)

Typeset by Type Study, Scarborough
Printed in Great Britain by St Edmundsbury Press, Bury St Edmunds,
Suffolk

For Pam
Who has expanded my horizons,
brought better understanding
and provided great support

Contents

Acknowledgements

On the 1993 anniversary of the devastating battle of Guèrnica, I happened to be travelling in the Basque Country following a conference at the University of Navarre. The newspapers brought eerily reminiscent photos and accounts of new devastation and use of terror against civilian populations, this time in Sarajevo. Such juxtapositions bring insight, and the opportunity to discuss this recurrence of nationalist violence with wise travelling companions advanced my understanding more, I am sure, than my paper on nationalism and social change had helped anyone at the previous conference. Years of writing produce many such debts.

I began reflecting seriously on nationalism in response to experience in and study of Yugoslavia, China, and Norway. I owe much to scholars and others in each place. More recently, I have benefited from time spent in Eritrea, teaching at the University of Asmara, privileged to participate in some of the impressive deliberations of the Constitutional Commission, and able to discuss the struggle for national autonomy and the project of building a new nation with veterans of the liberation fronts, scholars, and a range of citizens. My wife, Pamela DeLargy, introduced me to Eritrea and has remained my most important interlocutor.

My ideas on nationalism grew largely while I was on the faculty of the University of North Carolina. Members of the Program in Social Theory and Cross-Cultural Studies were masters of constructive criticism. Team-teaching a course on nationalism with Lloyd Kramer was of immense value, as well as pleasure. Many students have also been important teachers, especially Steven Pfaff. Karen Albright ably prepared the index. My work – and colleagues

– as Director of the University Center for International Studies brought important stimulation. So did invitations to present work on nationalism elsewhere. Edward Tiryakian invited me more than once to his stimulating seminar at Duke University. Discussion following my Ross Lectures at UCLA and my Bridges Lecture and seminars at the University of Washington was especially valuable, and brought home weaknesses in early formulations. Work in progress also benefited from critique in seminars at Stockholm University, Uppsala University, Gothenberg University, Lund University, the University of Oslo, the Swedish Collegium for Advanced Study in Social Sciences, the University of Toronto, George Mason University, New York University, the University of California at Berkeley, Northwestern University, Rutgers University, Candido Mendes University, and the Center for Transcultural Studies – as well as the University of Navarre.

Introduction

Nationalism has been big news off and on for 200 years. Just as often, it has been declared passé. Nationalism figured in revolutions and wars of independence. But it was a measure of the very success of nationalist projects that the existence and political autonomy of nations could be taken for granted most of the time. At least in the rich Western countries, we tended to ignore the nationalism that was embedded in our entire view of the world – organizing citizenship and passports, the way we look at history, the way we divide up literatures and cinemas, the way we compete in the Olympic games. We focused on nationalism only when it appeared in the form of conflicts between states and those who would change their boundaries or systems of government. This kind of collective action – often violent – ebbed and flowed visibly; each ebb allowed scholars to imagine that nationalism was a problem from the past now rapidly fading away. But behind the overt nationalist struggles lay deeper patterns of collective identity and pride, given form by nationalism as a way of talking and thinking and seeing the world – a world made up at one basic level of nations and their international relations.

In the 1990s, nationalism became front page news again. The break-up of the Soviet Union encouraged nationalists in a dozen of its former parts to declare their autonomy. Trying to get political borders to match ethnic boundaries, Armenians and Azeris fought in Nagorno-Karabakh. Chechen rebels clashed with Russia itself. And right-wing Russian nationalists complained about the loss of their country's former dominions.

Nor was nationalist fighting limited to the former Soviet Union.

Serbian, Croatian and Bosnian neighbours began killing each other in what was once Yugoslavia. More peacefully, Czechoslovakia split into the Czech Republic and Slovakia. Quebec came within a percentage point of voting to secede from Canada. Norwegian voters expressed their nationalist sentiments by rejecting membership of the European Union. Some argued that the EU was itself beginning to advocate Europeanness as a new nationalism – just as it was building a new state-like apparatus. Great Britain gave up one more of its claims to empire by ceding its colony of Hong Kong to China in the name of national sovereignty (even though this was anything but self-determination for the citizens of Hong Kong). American politicians competed with each other to prove their nationalist credentials by taking tough stands on immigration or on trade with Asia. Iraq invaded Kuwait, claiming the erstwhile province of colonial Iraq to be an integral part of the nation; the United Nations defended the national sovereignty of a Kuwaiti regime that constituted a minority of the country's inhabitants. In the same Middle East, when Palestinians' long pursuit of an autonomous national state finally began to bear tangible fruit, an Israeli prime minister was murdered by an ultra-nationalist Jew. Eritrea became an independent state after 30 years of nationalist struggle with an Ethiopia that was first explicitly an empire and then the object of a brutal communist effort at nation making. The new government of Ethiopia in turn boldly sought to pre-empt potential nationalist rebellions by offering a constitutional guarantee of the right to autonomy and even potential secession for its diverse constituent nationalities. Farther south, the African National Congress brought majority rule to South Africa. But in the Sudan, northerners killed southern separatists in the name of national unity.

The litany of examples could go on, powerful testimony to the continued currency of nationalism. In one sense, however, it is misleading. To look only at these often violent struggles encourages us to imagine that nationalism is simply a problem to be remedied, an issue that will fade as soon as borders are clarified and popular sovereignty established. This would be to forget the extent to which borders and popular sovereignty themselves are part of the nationalist discourse by which we give conceptual form and practical organization to the modern world. Nationalism is significant not only in crises and overt conflicts. It is basic to collective identity in the modern era, and to the specific form of state which has predominated for the last 200 years. Indeed, nationalism is not only a matter of politics, but of culture and personal identity. The discourse of nations is couched especially in terms of passion and identification, while that of states – kindred in many ways – is phrased more in terms of reason and interests. Nationalism has emotional power partly because it helps to make us who we are, because it inspires artists and composers, because it gives us a link with history (and thus with immortality). Witness the nationalism in this review of a London exhibition of works 'saved by the National Art Collections Fund' (itself conceived during the mid-nineteenth-century 'Springtime of Nations'): 'Simply put, the central question is whether an ancient nation has the will and the financial means to retain the works of art necessary for the survival of its past and the continuity of its culture' (Melikian 1997: 7). Still more simply put, during the Falklands War (to give the conflict its English name), I visited Frank Harris, a worker from my Oxford college who was in the hospital dying of emphysema. 'People die', he said, 'but there'll always be an England'.

Nationalism comes in manifold forms, some benign and reassuring and others terrifying. Social scientists have sometimes been tempted to try to analyze 'good' nationalism, or patriotism, and 'bad' nationalism, or chauvinism, as though they were completely different social phenomena. This makes each hard to understand, however, and obscures their commonalities. Both positive and negative manifestations of national identity and loyalty are shaped by the common discourse of nationalism. None of the particular cases can be understood fully without seeing how a more global – indeed *inter*national – rhetoric has helped to produce and give form to each. This goes for nationalist movements, nationalist state policies, nationalist traditions in literature and the arts, and ordinary people's everyday conceptions of where and how they fit into the world. Nationalism is, among other things, what Michel Foucault (1969, 1977; see also Brennan 1990) called a 'discursive formation', a way of speaking that shapes our consciousness, but also is problematic enough that it keeps generating more issues and questions, keeps propelling us into further talk, keeps producing debates over how to think about it.

The issue is not only whether participants use a specific term (cf. Greenfeld 1992). It is, rather, whether participants use a rhetoric, a way of speaking, a kind of language that carries with it connections to other events and actions, that enables or disables certain other ways of speaking or acting, or that is recognized by others as entailing certain consequences. When Quebecois partisans use the rhetoric of nationalism, for example, they make implicit reference to anti-imperialist nationalisms, they inhibit those who might espouse joining with the United States or France, and they lay a claim to legitimacy as a potentially autonomous state.

Recognition as a nation clearly requires social solidarity – some level of integration among the members of the ostensible nation, and collective identity – the recognition of the whole by its members, and a sense of individual self that includes membership in the whole. But social solidarity and collective identity can exist in many sorts of groupings, from families to employees of business corporations to imperial armies. They are minimal conditions for calling a population a nation, but far from a definition. What additional characteristics should ideally also be present for us to call a population with social solidarity and collective identity a nation?

This is where the discursive formation of nationalism comes in. This way of thinking about social solidarity, collective identity, and related questions (like political legitimacy) plays a crucial role both in the production of nationalist self-understandings and the recognition of nationalist claims by others. It is in this sense that Benedict Anderson has described nations as 'imagined communities'. As he says, 'all communities larger than primordial villages of face-to-face contact (and perhaps even these) are imagined. Communities are to be distinguished, not by their falsity–genuineness, but by the style in which they are imagined' (1991: 6). There are other ways of distinguishing communities, of course, such as their scale, extent of administrative organization, degree of internal equality, and so forth. But our first task is indeed to get some grasp of the distinctive form of 'imagining' collective identity and social solidarity that is associated with nationalism.

The following features of the rhetoric of nation seem most important, though none of them is precisely definitive and each may be present in greater or lesser degree in any nation. It is the pattern formed by having a preponderance of them that is crucial:

1 Boundaries, of territory, population, or both.
2 Indivisibility – the notion that the nation is an integral unit.
3 Sovereignty, or at least the aspiration to sovereignty, and thus

formal equality with other nations, usually as an autonomous and putative self-sufficient state.

4 An 'ascending' notion of legitimacy – i.e. the idea that government is just only when supported by popular will or at least when it serves the interests of 'the people' or 'the nation'.

5 Popular participation in collective affairs – a population mobilized on the basis of national membership (whether for war or civic activities).

6 Direct membership, in which each individual is understood to be immediately a part of the nation and in that respect categorically equivalent to other members.

7 Culture, including some combination of language, shared beliefs and values, habitual practices.

8 Temporal depth – a notion of the nation as such existing through time, including past and future generations, and having a history.

9 Common descent or racial characteristics.

10 Special historical or even sacred relations to a certain territory.

Note again that these are features of the rhetoric of nation, claims that are commonly made in describing nations. Nations cannot be defined effectively by empirical measures of whether they are actually able to achieve sovereignty, to maintain integrity by defending themselves against internal splits, or to enforce sharp boundaries, by whether their culture is perfectly unified or particularly ancient. Rather, nations are constituted largely by the claims themselves, by the way of talking and thinking and acting that relies on these sorts of claims to produce collective identity, to mobilize people for collective projects, and to evaluate peoples and practices.

There is no perfect list; we are identifying a common pattern, not a precise definition of nation. The points listed can help us to develop an 'ideal type,' but this is an aid to conceptualization, not an operational definition or an empirically testable description. The word 'nation' is used sensibly and commonly understood when it is applied to populations which have or claim most of the characteristics listed. Which six, or seven, or eight characteristics will be most important will vary from nation to nation. Recognition of nations works not by discerning the 'essence' of nationhood, but through what Ludwig Wittgenstein (1953) called a pattern of 'family resemblance'. Some siblings may have the family nose without the family jaw, or the family's characteristic green eyes without its characteristic high forehead; none of the features is shared among all the members of the family without also being shared with others who are not part of the family. Yet we can see the pattern. National ideology in any one setting may lack one or more of its characteristic features, or place greater or lesser emphasis on others. Recognition as a nation is not based on strict definition, but on a preponderance of this pattern.[1]

Nationalism, in this sense, has three dimensions. First, there is nationalism as discourse: the production of a cultural understanding and rhetoric which leads people throughout the world to think and frame their aspirations in terms of the idea of nation and national identity, and the production of particular versions of nationalist thought and language in particular settings and traditions. Second, there is nationalism as project: social movements and state policies by which people attempt to advance the interests of collectivities they understand as nations, usually pursuing in some combination (or in a historical progression) increased participation in an existing state, national autonomy, independence and self-determination, or the amalgamation of territories. Third, there is nationalism as evaluation: political and cultural ideologies that claim superiority for a particular nation; these are often associated with movements or state policies, but need not be. In this third sense, nationalism is often given the status of an ethical imperative: national boundaries *ought* to coincide with state boundaries, for example; members of a nation *ought* to conform to its moral values, etc. It is through some of the actions that follow from these ethical imperatives that nationalism comes to be associated with *excesses* of loyalty to one's nation – as in ethnic cleansing, ideologies of national purification, and hostility to foreigners.

Loyalty to one's own group is certainly of ancient origins. It is the dimension of nationalism that has the clearest claim to be primordial, to have existed since before memory, before human history was recorded. But groups and group loyalty can take many forms and hardly constitute or explain nationalism by themselves. One can be loyal to a family – a much more common loyalty through history than that involved in nationalism – or to a city, whether or not the city is considered part of a nation. Machiavelli's loyalty to Florence in the sixteenth century is part of the history of nationalism because it led him to write extensively and influentially on the nature of the state, on political rule, and on the relationship that binds individual members of political communities to their rulers. But sixteenth-century Florence was not a nation, and neither was the relationship of the identity 'Florentine' to the broader 'Italian' decisive for Machiavelli or fully worked out in his time. It was not until the nineteenth-century 'Risorgimento' that the 'nationalist' idea of unifying all Italians under a single state gained widespread currency. Even then, the ideology was ahead of the reality. As Massimo D'Azeglio worried: 'We have made Italy, now we have to make Italians' (Hobsbawm 1990: 44).

Such a programme suggests the promotion of an internally homogeneous national identity. This is the domestic mirror image of the notion of external differences. The idea that each people has an 'essential' identity – internally unified and different from all others – is an important thread in the history of nationalism. Such a notion can easily turn oppressive, and indeed it figures in both 'ethnic cleansing' and the project of encouraging 'correct' culture and behaviour among those who are deemed parts of the nation. There is an important distinction between webs of interpersonal solidarity and demands for oneness with broad categories of ostensibly similar people.

In what was becoming England in 1066, thus, it was one thing to be loyal to one's king and kinsmen when faced with Norman invaders. It was quite another, in the years that followed, to nurture English nationalism by mythologizing Camelot, making the 'Norman Yoke' the focus of quasi-class complaint, and proclaiming that 'there will always be an England'. Loyalty to the abstract category England was quite different from loyalty to one's actual and specific comrades. A web of interpersonal relationships locates a person locally, but membership in the category 'nation' locates people in a complex, globally integrated world. It cannot be dismissed lightly. At the same time, it is a source of conflicts and an often problematic way of dealing with personal and collective grievances.

* * *

In the first chapter, we shall explore further the meaning of nation and nationalism, emphasizing the 'discursive formation' that has helped to structure the whole modern era, providing a common rhetoric to diverse movements and policies. One of the major debates in the literature on nationalism is between those who see it as simply an extension of ancient ethnic identities and those who see it as distinctively modern. In presenting nationalism as a discursive formation with several different dimensions, I shall argue that though some features are much older than others, the pattern we now recognize as nationalism is distinctive to the modern era. The second chapter will develop this theme by comparing nationalism to ethnicity and both to kinship as ways of organizing ('imagining') social solidarity and collective identity. The content of different nationalisms may draw on ethnicity, but it is transformed by the discourse of nationalism and not a full explanation either of that discourse or of the pattern of actual nationalisms. A closely related question is whether nationalism should be understood primarily as inherited or invented, as primordial or constructed – and how we should understand the ways in which nationalisms invoke (and sometimes manipulate) history. We shall examine this in the third chapter, where I shall argue that the literature presents us with an unnecessarily dichotomous choice, that 'primordiality' may be constructed and relatively new without losing its force or significance. The fourth chapter will explore how nationalism figured in the formation of a new kind of political community linked to the rise of the modern state. The fifth chapter will take up the tension between universal and parochial themes in nationalism, the contrast between reliance on 'civic' and ethnic conceptions of national membership, and the transformations wrought by constituting the local as a token of more universal type. The sixth chapter will consider nationalism in relation to imperialism, colonialism, and economic globalization, and examine the ways in which 'domestic' nationalisms depend on and are shaped by being located in a world of nations and nation-states.

For better or worse, this book will not offer a comprehensive theory of nationalism. Nationalism is a rhetoric for speaking about too many different things for a single theory to explain it – let alone to explain each of those different movements, cultural patterns, state policies or other projects shaped in part by the rhetoric of nationalism. This does not mean that theory is not needed, but rather that grasping nationalism in its multiplicity of forms requires multiple theories. To address a question like, 'Why do nationalist movements seem to come in waves?' will require a different theory from the question, 'Why is nationalist ideology pervasively bound up with sexuality and gender?' Yet dealing adequately with either question will call for a more general grasp – partly theoretical, partly historical – of the discursive formation of nationalism and its structuring influence and emotional power in the modern world.

1

The Modernity and Diversity of Nationalisms

There was no first nationalist. Neither was there any single moment at which people who previously had no idea of nation and no political aspirations or ideological preferences for their own country suddenly began to think in nationalist terms. Rather, several different threads of historical change came together to produce modern nationalism. It is a fruitless exercise to try to 'explain' nationalism (and cognate ideas like nation and national identity) by searching for the first example and then studying the spread of terminology or practices. The term 'nation' is old (though 'nationalism' is relatively new), but before the modern era, it meant only people linked by place of birth and culture.[1] It signalled nothing about the relationship of such identity to larger or smaller groupings; neither did it carry clear political connotations.

The first examples of modern nationalism have been identified variously as appearing in the tensions that led to the English Civil War (Greenfeld 1992), in Latin American independence movements (Anderson 1991), in the French Revolution (Best 1988; Alter 1989), and in German reaction and Romanticism (Breuilly 1993; Kedourie 1994). These differences cannot be settled empirically; they reflect slightly varying definitions. For our purposes, it suffices to indicate that by the end of the eighteenth century, in the French Revolution and its wake, the discursive formation was fully in play. How much earlier this was so will remain subject to dispute, though before the modern era there was no point at which most of these dimensions were simultaneously important. Most dimensions, or threads in the fabric of nationalist discourse, have an older history of their own. And of course, some modern countries have histories before the discourse of nationalism, though these are only retro-spectively constituted as *national* histories (Armstrong 1982). The English nation, thus, is rooted in Anglo-Saxon history and shaped by the Norman Conquest. Conflicts among England, Scotland and Wales helped give each a distinctive identity. But the England (not Britain, as it happens, though both Welshmen and Scots fought) that Henry V took into war against France became an object of properly nationalist discourse with later claims on the memory of Agincourt in new political and social contexts. It was Shakespeare and later historians who made 'King Harry' a nationalist, and even then incompletely.

Nationalism, and the modern sense of 'nation', cannot be under-stood entirely in terms of the cultural distinctiveness of various nations, nor of the modern states that have given nationalism its most distinctive political significance. Long-existing cultural pat-terns have contributed to national identities, but the meaning and form of these cultural patterns has been transformed in the modern era. Though the cultural 'content' of nations is important, it cannot fully explain them. State formation was the single most important factor in changing the form and significance of cultural variations (though the extension of market and production relations and other factors also mattered a great deal). State formation brought citizen armies, increased administrative unification, road building, linguistic standardization, popular educational systems, occasions for popular political participation, and many other changes that helped produce a new consciousness of national identity. But states did not simply create nations.

It would be a mistake to be drawn into debate over whether cul-tural or material factors were primary. Both were crucial and appeared in indistinguishable ways. Indeed, as John Meyer and col-leagues have emphasized, the modern form of state is itself 'an institution that is essentially cultural in nature' (Thomas and Meyer 1984: 461). Innovations like citizen armies and state-run edu-cational, welfare, or taxation systems are *ideas* that can be shared in a global cultural flow, as well as material patterns of activity. Nationalist discourse is one of the most important elements of this global cultural flow, and it has both transformed ethnicity and cul-tural patterns and shaped the process of state formation itself. National identity was thus not simply already available to give states their boundaries or to be used by political leaders. Though it had older roots, it was shaped by the process of state making, including wars, as well as by markets and transport and communications infrastructures. At the same time, the development and spread of nationalist discourse is not reducible to state formation or political manipulation; it has autonomous significance, appears in cultural arenas not directly defined by state-making projects, and has often informed popular action to reform or resist patterns of state making. The key is to focus on nation as a 'form', and not merely on the 'content' of various national identities.

The culture of any particular country may show more or less continuity over time, and may be more or less integrated and uniform. But nationalism is a way of constructing identity that does not address such variation so much as it simply posits temporal depth and internal integration. The intellectual historian Elie Kedourie came close to this approach with his classic definition of nationalism:

> Nationalism is a doctrine invented in Europe at the beginning of the nineteenth century. It pretends to supply a criterion for the determination of the unit of population proper to enjoy a government exclusively its own, for the legitimate exercise of power in the state, and for the right organization of a society of states. Briefly, the doctrine holds that humanity is naturally divided into nations, that nations are known by certain characteristics which can be ascertained, and that the only legitimate type of government is national self-government.
>
> (Kedourie 1994: 1)

Nationalism is not just a doctrine, however, but a more basic way of talking, thinking, and acting. To limit nationalism simply to a political doctrine – or, in Gellner's (1983: 5) pithy summary, 'a political principle, which holds that the political and the national unit should be congruent' – is to narrow our understanding of it too much. It doesn't do justice to the extent to which nationalism and national identities shape our lives outside of explicitly political concerns – and especially outside competition over the structuring of state boundaries. Writers may be concerned with having 'national' readerships, not with whether these readers have state power. The nationalism of soccer fans may sometimes have political implications, but it does not stem entirely from political sources. Aboriginal groups may use nationalist rhetoric to seek special recognition without seeking to form states or to secede – whether from Canada or South Africa. Why exclude these?

This more general imbrication of nationalism in our lives gives nationalism part of its political power. We are nationalists in our pride and in our only partly economically motivated desires to keep out foreign products (while our country sells its abroad). People respond to nationalist messages – from flags and ceremonies to explicit appeals for us to take up arms and kill on behalf of our countries – for reasons deeper than doctrine. This is also why nationalism doesn't lose its force – even in law courts – just because researchers are able to show that as doctrine it fails adequately to perform the jobs Kedourie describes, shaping and furthering conflicts between rival nationalisms rather than settling them objectively. As a way of imagining communities, in Anderson's phrase, and thereby giving collective identities actual form, nationalism may be problematic or misleading, but it is not simply right or wrong, any more than individualism, or bilateral descent, or the use of money can be simply right or wrong. These are ways of constructing the social reality we live, which we can regret or compare unfavourably to other possibilities or wish to change, but which do not admit of simple right/wrong judgments.

Kedourie is right that nationalism is modern (though we could quibble about precise dating). It is not just recent, it is one of the definitive features of the modern era. This is the era in which the discourse of nationalism has become all but universal, and has been linked closely to the practical power and administrative capacities of states (just as it is the era of capitalism, global interconnection, and technological innovation). But it is also crucial to recognize that nationalism works, in part, because national identities and the whole rhetoric of nationalism appear commonly to people as though they were always already there, ancient, or even natural.

Mapping modernity

Most of the time, we tend to think of nations as given. We have an image of the world as divided into different 'peoples', each of which has its own cultural identity and its own country – though we know that some people live outside their native or 'natural' countries. This image is reinforced when we travel: we show passports and cross immigration checkpoints; we pay customs duties and fill out forms that ask us our nationality. Even when we stay at home, the idea of nations is basic to our mental picture of the world as a map.

But the globe has not always been divided into the patchwork quilt of differently coloured countries shown on today's maps. Making maps this way, with sharp borders between countries and an attempt at a 'bird's eye' view from above, is a modern practice.[2] Most earlier maps were either local – like city plans or charts of shorelines – or focused on directions for travellers, featuring roads between cities and natural landmarks like mountains, and offering much vaguer representations of who lived where, without the attempt to define boundaries precisely. Attempts to represent the world as a whole were few, though pioneering efforts were made by some Greeks in the era of the Roman empire. Maps tended to look outward from centres of power – whether these were at Rome or the ancient Chinese capital of Xi'an.

Map-making actually declined dramatically in Western Europe after the fall of the Roman Empire. Byzantium and parts of the Arab world retained knowledge of the ancient Greek skills, and these were reintroduced to Western Europe in the Renaissance. Advances in cartographic technique were renewed in the fifteenth century, sparked by the rediscovery of Ptolomaic geometry and the development of new techniques of projection of curves onto flat surfaces. The idea that the earth was round gained credence. Renaissance maps once again represented the world as a whole, grasping in improved ways the relationships of the continents and oceans. Aided and stimulated by the voyages of exploration, European maps offered improved knowledge not only of physical geography but of the location of different peoples and empires. Map-making grew to help navigators and to report on their discoveries. But modern maps also reflected a transformation both in how the world was understood and in how power was socially organized.

In the seventeenth and especially the eighteenth centuries, maps began commonly to represent the world as divided neatly into territories with clear borders rather than vague frontiers. This reflected not only the Enlightenment passion for clarity but the increasing division of the world into the dominions of different European states, and the closely related policing and even militarization of borders. The idea of a world divided naturally into discrete nations, each linked to a distinctive political unit or state, was central to this transformation.

First and foremost, European states grew stronger. They gained increased political and military power, and used it in conflicts that both unified the territories under their control and created relatively stable oppositions to neighbouring countries. Where rulers mobilized citizen armies (instead of using mercenaries), the people they ruled gained a stronger sense of their common identity and distinction from their neighbours. Map-making and nationalism reflected both the new internal unity and the clearer borders. The turning point came with the Napoleonic Wars. Napoleon did not simply attempt to acquire new territory in the manner of traditional dynastic combatants. He sought to transform the social and political organization of conquered countries. At first he was an apostle of the Republicanism of the French Revolution. Later he declared himself emperor, but still saw his influence as modernizing, not simply Gallicizing. One of the central themes in the ideology that Napoleon sought to spread was increasing citizen participation – not least in Napoleon's armies, but also in politics and culture. The Napoleonic Wars were thus crucial to sparking national consciousness throughout Europe. Not only did they unite many groups in opposition to the French, they encouraged the construction of both this opposition and the domestic political and cultural institutions of various countries on the 'national' model. In their wake, governments deployed reconnaissance surveys to gather better geographic information and attempted with renewed energy to have their borders represented clearly on maps.

Second, these states sought to complement their military power by domestic administrative capacity. This started with tax collection, which among other things financed the wars and included conscription for military service.[3] Leaders wanted more precise information about the countries under their control. Accordingly, they sponsored surveys designed to gain clearer knowledge of the lie of the land and its use. British governments were pioneers in this, drawing on cadastral maps – those designed to show patterns of land use and property holding, often along with other factors of economic and administrative relevance – as early as the sixteenth century to aid their colonization of Ireland. Especially from the eighteenth century, the domestic integration of nation-states by markets, transport, and intensified central government administration made the use of cadastral maps increasingly commonplace. This effort grew alongside the development of censuses and related efforts to count and describe the inhabitants, and alongside the building of better roads, then railways, and better communications systems (which along with more popular education helped to encourage standardization of national languages). All of this fostered national integration, making it meaningful for a map to treat France, say, as a single unit rather than focusing on the divisions among various feudal duchies and baronies.

Third, Europeans devoted increasing energy to colonizing the rest of the world. This meant not only finding out who and what was in the rest of the world and how to get around, but establishing power and proprietary rights. Even where the early work of imperialism was done largely by private enterprise, states soon followed, dividing the world into the territories of different European powers (especially, for example, in the late-nineteenth-century 'scramble' for Africa). Some of the earliest recognizably modern maps describe the eighteenth-century division of North America into the dominions of different European states. The European colonizers organized their overseas possessions into colonies modelled partly on European nation-states. They thus consolidated previously dispersed principalities (as the British did in India), established centralized capitals, and built transport and communications systems (which among other things facilitated military rule). They developed new educational systems in which European languages (and learning) often knitted together countries divided by local languages and dialects. Spreading their own European languages for official purposes (as well as cultural imperialism), they created new capacities for communication across ethnic boundaries.

Finally, map-making reflected technological changes and the growth of science. Better geometry went into developing workable representations of the curved earth on flat paper. Telescopes gave surveyors better measurements. Perhaps above all, hot air balloons and aeroplanes gave map-makers the 'bird's eye' view from which to represent the world as seen from above rather than from the perspective of a traveller on the surface. These new technologies went hand in hand with the pursuit of precision, and furthered the development of an idea of neatly divided territories, whose borders distinguished not only governments but cultures, each presumed to be discrete. The printed word helped to encourage internal standardization of language and, with mass readerships in the nineteenth century, of other features of increasingly 'national' cultures. Aided by new printing techniques, maps also became more widely available and more a part of the construction of everyday consciousness both of one's own country and of its situation in relation to the rest of the world-system of nation-states.

Changes in map-making have continued up to the present day – for example with satellite photography. But this is not a book about map-making. The point of this example is to call attention to how maps came to represent the world as a world of nation-states. The countries they delimit sharply from each other exist as political, social, and cultural creations. They are not given by the physical nature of the world – as can be seen by comparing a 'political' map that distinguishes countries with a map that uses colours and other devices to represent patterns of vegetation or rainfall or elevation instead of nation-state boundaries. The countries on the political maps all got their boundaries through at least potentially traceable historical events; they are not 'primordial' (dating from before history). Neither are they historically permanent; though they may be of varying antiquity, they can change. Yet we tend to treat these nation-states as part of the given character of the world. They are always already there, taken as established conditions for our conventional inquiries into how they should be governed, the structure or solidarity of their populations and the character of their cultures. They are the units from which the United Nations receives representatives and the units for which it – like the World Bank and other organizations – gathers statistics.

Maps now typically represent the entire world as a world of nation-states. The technique was standard by the nineteenth century, but in a sense, the whole globe was filled in only quite recently. Independence from European colonial rule was part of the story – and though a few exceptions remain, this was mainly complete by the 1960s. There were also some non-European colonialists, of course, like Ethiopia, which attempted to rule Eritrea until 1991. Perhaps most symbolically, the Soviet Union was in a sense an 'anti-national state'. Maps portraying global population, economic, health or other patterns commonly represented the Soviet Union as a large, blank space. This reflected lack of data and uncertainty about the status of the separate republics that made it up. It also aptly symbolized the last major holdout against the division of the world into national states. While its rulers sometimes tried to mobilize nationalist sentiments to their own advantage, and while much Soviet policy represented a Russian national dominance over other nationalities within the country, the Soviet Union also marked an attempt to keep the territory of a multinational empire unified. Communism was, in this sense as much as in that of a socialized economy, an alternative ideology to that of the West. For the West was committed to a vision of capitalism involving political autonomy for nation-states engaged in more or less free trade, both domestically and internationally. After the Soviet Union collapsed, advocates of a variety of nationalities rushed to claim autonomy and demand representation at the UN and on the world's maps. The example reminds us that while nationalism is often rooted in old identities, it is also occasioned by new opportunities and pressures, and facilitated by the availability of an international rhetoric within which to shape claims both for the world's attention and the loyalty of citizens.

Most maps are shaped heavily – perhaps too heavily – by the experience and orientation of Europeans. This is why standard maps place Europe at the centre. The surface of the globe has no logical geographic centre; for those who made the maps, Europe was the social, cultural, and political centre. Most of us have seen maps that criticize this Eurocentric view by putting Australia at the top or Africa in the centre or representing the continents in proportion to their true geographical areas (the conventional projections make Europe and North America look larger than they really are). But we need also to develop critical self-awareness with regard to how maps lead us to take nation-states as given, and fixed, and as the obvious way in which the world should be represented. The globe has only been organized as a world-system of supposedly equivalent nation-states for a couple of hundred years. Before that, many local communities were not closely tied into or involved with the political affairs of what we now think of as 'their countries'. At the other extreme of scale, empires organized political life on a scale beyond the boundaries of most contemporary states. Even today, there are other important bases of identity and solidarity that don't fit with the nation-state model – religion, for example, particularly for those, like many Islamists, who reject the distinction of religious and secular authority and seek to create unified religious states. There are important internal differences within countries that the notion of a shared national culture can obscure. Especially with international migrations of a new scope, there are many people with multiple and cross-cutting 'national' identities.

As Chris Hann (1995: 123) remarks, 'the demarcation of cultures through precise lines on a map, as required by nationalism, is an awkward if not impossible exercise'. It is, of course, not only cultures that are hard to demarcate precisely with lines on a map. Economic relations also run across national boundaries and – at least for some citizens – so do personal relationships. While these lines have sharp meaning for certain political purposes, they are ambiguous for others.

Essentialism

Nationalism was not the whole, but only the most important part, of the tacit consensus forged in the late nineteenth century as to what would count as politically appropriate identities. It played a central role in the development of 'essentialist' thinking that was also basic to the way race, gender, sexual orientation and other sorts of collective identities came to be constituted (Calhoun 1995: Chapter 8). 'Essentialism' refers to a reduction of the diversity in a population to some single criterion held to constitute its defining 'essence' and most crucial character. This is often coupled with the claim that the 'essence' is unavoidable or given by nature. It is common to assume that these cultural categories address really existing and discretely identifiable collections of people. More surprisingly, many also assume that it is possible to understand each category – Germans, say, or women, Blacks, or gays – by focusing solely on its primary identifier rather than on the way it overlaps with, contests and/or reinforces others.

Put another way, it has been the tacit assumption of modern social and cultural thought that people are normally members of one and only one nation, that they are members of one and only one race, one gender, and one sexual orientation, and that each of these memberships describes neatly and concretely some aspect of their being.[4] It has been assumed that people naturally live in one world at a time, that they inhabit one way of life, that they speak one language, and that they themselves, as individuals, are singular, integral beings. All these assumptions came clearly into focus by the late nineteenth century, and all seem problematic.

Two further guiding assumptions in much modern thinking on matters of identity are that individuals ideally ought to achieve maximally integrated identities, and that to do so they need to inhabit self-consistent, unitary cultures or lifeworlds. This is one of the reasons why nationalist leaders commonly argue that in order to be fully free as individuals, people need their nation to be autonomous. It is thought normal for people to live in one culture at a time, for example; to speak one language; to espouse one set of values; to adhere to one polity. But why? Not, I would suggest, on the basis of historical or comparative evidence. On the contrary, throughout history and still to a considerable extent today we find multilingualism common; we find people moved simultaneously by different visions of the world (not least, religion and science); we find people able to understand themselves as members of very differently organized collectivities from families to communities, states or provinces, nations, and international organizations, and to recognize themselves through different identities at different times or stages of life. Civilization has flourished in polyglot and more heterogeneous empires and in cosmopolitan trading cities. Indeed, nationalist visions of internally uniform and sharply bounded cultural and political identities often have to be produced or maintained by struggle against a richer, more diverse and more promiscuously cross-cutting play of differences and similarities.

Modernity, ironically, has brought both the attempt to 'clarify' and 'consolidate' identities, and the production of an enormously increased field of cultural differences – both by expanding the reach and communicative ease of interactions across lines of difference and by encouraging new freedoms in cultural creativity. It has been an era not of simple sameness but of conflicting tendencies. The idea that people need 'naturally' to feel at home in a taken-for-granted and internally homogeneous community contends with the creation of polities and cultural fields too large and differentiated to be organized as single communities. Home, it has famously been said, is the place where they always have to take you in. In an important sense, it is this sense of having a home that many people derive from ideas of membership in a nation. Even when this sense of having a home is not immediately tied to any specific 'nationalist' political project, it is a powerful facilitator of such projects; it paves the way for mobilizing people in solidarity with the rest of 'their' nation; it encourages an identification with one's nation that makes it attractive to think of it as superior because that implies a certain superiority for oneself. In this regard, the politics of nationalism are always as much domestic – about conforming to authoritative images of nationality – as international. It is not, therefore, an adequate response to human differences to allow each person to find the group within which he or she feels at home. There is no doubt that a sense of being at home is very attractive. But it needs at least to be balanced with the virtues of a public space for mutual engagement across lines of difference, within national groups as well as between them.[5]

In the late nineteenth century, precisely as the globalization of political and economic organization and the worldwide flows of culture were reaching unprecedented levels, the urge to organize social life in terms of sharp boundaries, national identities, and essentialist cultural categories likewise reached a peak. In Europe, it was in this period that nationalists began effectively to urge immigration controls; in this period they created the standing citizen armies that fought World War I; in this period they opposed socialism, in part, precisely because it was internationalist (Hobsbawm 1990: 123). It was in this period that modern anti-Semitism took shape. And it was in this period that nationalism became most conclusively identified, in the European context, with movements for secession rather than amalgamation of existing states (Carr 1945: 24–5). No era placed greater emphasis on the autonomy of the nation-state or the capacity of the idea of nation to define large-scale collective identities. But it did so precisely when and partly because the world was becoming pronouncedly international. In this there may lie some lesson for the present era when the acceleration of global processes of capital accumulation, the rapid global transfer of technology, the almost instantaneous spread of cultural products, and huge waves of migration lead many to imagine that the nation-state is likely to vanish quickly into the shadows of history.

Complex phenomenon, multiple causes

Researchers have attempted many explanations of nationalism. It has been explained as the result of enduring ethnic identities (Geertz 1963; Smith 1986; Hutcheson 1994); of the political and cultural changes associated with industrialization (Gellner 1964, 1983); of separatist responses to unequal economic development on the part of those at the periphery of an integrated economy and state (Hechter 1975); of the status anxiety and *ressentiment* of new elites claiming distinction from older elites or from their neighbours (Greenfeld 1992); and of the invention of an ideology to legitimate states within capitalist economic relations (Hobsbawm 1990) or to reinforce centralization and unification associated with state building (Tilly 1975, 1990; Mann 1993, 1995). All these factors and others have contributed to the creation of nationalist movements and the currency of nationalist discourse. None of them explains them entirely. Indeed, to treat any one of them as a 'master variable' explaining nationalism makes an account reductionistic. Such an account fails to grapple with all that we might reasonably consider nationalism, reducing nationalism arbitrarily to something else, usually something smaller – if more easily measurable. These factors explain various *contents* of nationalism or *processes* associated with nationalism, but they do not explain the form of nation or nationalist discourse itself.

Studies emphasizing these various specific 'causes' or 'independent variables' may be illuminating, but they are not adequate to grasping the more general way nationalism shapes the modern world. Although part of their attraction is their apparent causal parsimony, they do not cumulate in a general theory or a single history of nationalism.[6] This is so most basically because they address heterogeneous objects of analysis. At the level of practical activity, there are many diverse nationalisms; the idea of nation is integral to many different aspects of how we understand the world, to sharply contrasting state policies, and to widely varying social movements. Explanations of each case must draw on at least partially different variables, rooted in specific histories and other causal factors such as the politics of state elites or the dynamics of social movements. Structural factors, from the growth of state power to the globalization of capitalism, may create conditions that nationalist discourse is used to grasp. But use of the discourse of nationalism is partially autonomous from these specific instances and contributing factors, and links otherwise disparate phenomena in significant ways.

An enormous range of otherwise different movements, ideologies, policies, and conflicts are constituted in part through the use of terms like 'nation', 'national', 'nationality', 'nation-state', and 'national interest'. The common denominator among, say, Japanese economic protectionism, Serbian ethnic cleansing, Americans singing the 'Star-Spangled Banner' before baseball games, and the

way the World Bank collects statistics is a discursive form that
shapes and links all of them, even though it may not offer a full
causal explanation of any of them. Thus Breton separatism, pan-
Arab nationalism and the declarations of Chinese student protest-
ers that they were willing to die for the future of China each arise
in different historical trajectories and from different circumstances,
but are joined by the use of a common rhetoric. They may also be
joined by other common denominators, but none of these by itself
defines them as 'nationalisms'. They are all influenced, thus, by
some sense of resentment at the strength, wealth or privileges
enjoyed by other groups. The power of modern states shapes each.
But these do not define them as instances of nationalism.

Any time a political leader uses the rhetoric of nationalism –
rather, for example, than that of communist internationalism – this
has significance. When a peasant rebellion claims to represent a
repressed nation, this is significantly different from relying on the
language of class alone – or of religion. When a novelist (or painter
or composer) presents his or her work as embodying the spirit of
the nation, this is different from presenting it as the work of a root-
less genius or cosmopolitan citizen of the world. It is impossible to
define the commonalities of these diverse forms of nationalism by
a single explanatory variable – such as state building, industrialization, unequal economic development, or *ressentiment*. What is
general is the *discourse* of nationalism. It does not completely
explain any specific such activity or event, but it helps to constitute
each through cultural framing.

Gellner (1983: 55) recognizes some of the power of such framing
when he stresses the extent to which 'it is nationalism which en-
genders nations, and not the other way round'. This is much like my
suggestion here that we treat nationalism first as a discursive formation. Gellner is concerned to argue against a simple ethnic deter-
minism: 'For every effective nationalism, there are *n* potential ones,
groups defined either by shared culture inherited from the agrarian
world or by some other link ... which *could* give hope of establishing a homogeneous industrial community, but which neverthe-
less do not bother to struggle, which fail to activate their potential
nationalism, which do not even try' (1983: 45). But in following this
lead, we need to be careful not to imply that nations are created
simply to satisfy the political principle of nationalism (cf. Hobsbawm and Ranger 1983). This would suggest, as Anderson (1991)

has complained, that the nations thus invoked are somehow purely arbitrary creations of ideology, less than fully real. Instead, we need to see the discourse of nationalism as multidimensional. Ethnicity is only one potential source of homogeneity and mutual obligation; while homogeneity and mutual obligation characterize many nations (or nationalist ideologies), they do not characterize all. People are also bound together (and divided) by state power and military might, participatory politics, and other institutional formations. Nations have multiple sources, including the discourse of nationalism itself.

Underestimating nationalism

Nearly 150 years ago, Karl Marx and Friedrich Engels wrote famously, 'Workers of the world, unite! You have nothing to lose but your chains!' The occasion was the wave of revolutionary movements that swept through Europe around 1848 in the wake of widespread economic crisis. Marx and Engels ([1848] 1974) coined their slogan as part of the Manifesto they wrote for the newly created (but short-lived) League of the Just – a first communist International. 'Communists of various nationalities have assembled in London', they wrote, 'and sketched the following manifesto to be published in the English, French, German, Italian, Flemish, and Danish languages'. Both the economic crisis and the revolutionary response had strongly international dimensions.

But Marx and Engels were wrong to think that workers of the world had nothing to lose but their chains, and also that most would agree to place membership of the workers of the world ahead of membership of their individual nations, religions, and other cultural or ethnic groupings. The 1848 revolutions, in fact, were the second wave of revolutions in which issues of economic rights, national autonomy, and the creation of participatory (not always properly democratic) political processes mingled. The first had come in the late eighteenth century, with the American and French Revolutions as its high points. It is worth pausing to emphasize that in each case these were international *waves*, and that the revolutions themselves had an international – as well as a nationalist – character. In 1776 and 1789, this can be symbolized by Tom Paine – the great English revolutionary democrat who wrote his *Defence of the Rights of Man* in the context of the American Revolution and who went on to be elected to the National Assembly of revolutionary France. Sixty years later, Europeans spoke of a 'Springtime of Nations', when it seemed that every oppressed people might gain self-expression and sovereignty (Kohn 1967; Meinecke 1970). In 1848 workers throughout Europe and in America lionized the struggles of Poles for national independence, making the name Kosciuszko briefly almost a household word. German tailors living in London sent money to help not only the Frankfurt Parliament but the French National Assembly. And after the German rebellion was crushed, the United States experienced its first large immigration of Germans.

The wave pattern continued after the mid-nineteenth century, with nationalist movements informing each other on an international scale, and in many cases linked to revolutions.[7] In the 1910s, World War I coincided with the break-up of the Austro-Hungarian Empire, and helped to launch both the Russian Revolution and the League of Nations. US president Wilson led the League's call for 'national self-determination' but this reflected as much as influenced the nationalist movements of the day. Just as the 'Young Europe' movement of the 1840s had been echoed immediately by 'Young Turks', the War and the fall of the Ottoman Empire brought the successful Turkish nationalist movement which gained control of the state in 1923 under Kemal Atattürk. Egyptian nationalism took modern form in the same period, though it struggled longer before comparable success and competed with Arab nationalism. These were crucial years too for nationalism in India, Korea and, with less emphasis on colonialism, in China.

The collapse of communism in 1989 helped to stimulate another international wave of nationalist movements. These occurred not only in formerly communist countries, but in a variety of places where a shifting international balance of power created new openings for insurgents (and the post-1989 flood of arms gave them new military strength).[8] Multiple factors go into explaining each of these waves. The collapse of empires and shifts in global balances of power were perhaps most important in giving nationalists the opportunity to act effectively (Gellner 1995: 6). Imperial collapse also made nationalism more attractive by reducing the capacity of imperial centres to deliver economic goods – and even simple safety and peace – to those they ruled. But the wave pattern is also influenced by international communications. Examples of nationalist insurgency – and success – spread by means of migrations, conferences, books, newspapers, radio, and – in the late twentieth century – television and even computer networks. The existence of some nationalist movements thus encourages the emergence of more and provides ideas and examples to each.

Crucially, this international discourse of nationalism helps to explain why people with grievances of a variety of sorts cast their struggles in the rhetorical framework of nationalism. The grievances may arise from economic, political, or cultural sources, but they do not produce insurgencies or social movements by themselves.[9] Welshmen unhappy with the underdevelopment of their country and their own material chances in life can choose to address their grievances and pursue their goals as readily through a class movement as through a nationalist one.[10] Indeed, class movements have found strong support among parts of the Welsh population – sometimes overlapping with nationalist thinking, sometimes quite separate from it. Likewise, one could argue that much of the spread of Welsh Methodism was motivated by the same grievances and concerns that have also informed working-class politics and Welsh nationalism. Why nationalism comes to dominate in those settings where it does – or for some people and not others within an ostensibly national population – are questions that by and large can be answered only within specific contexts, with knowledge of local history, of the nature of state (and other elite) power, and of what other potential or actual movements competed for allegiance.[11] But the availability and prominence of the discourse of nationalism is crucial, and it is a matter both of local history (not only of the potential insurgent nationalism but of the state that has dominated it) and of international communication.

The Soviet Union had long claimed to represent a special kind of internationalism and to have brought an end to nationalism and the historical conflict of nations in Eastern Europe and the Soviet Union. Writing in the state publisher Novosti's series on 'The Soviet Experience', for example, Nenarokov and Proskurin claimed that:

> as social antagonisms disappeared under socialism, so did national strife and racial inequality and oppression in every form. . . . The socialist multinational culture has been enriched through an intensive exchange of cultural and intellectual values. The socialist nations that have emerged in the USSR have formed a new historical community

of people – the Soviet people. . . . Today it would be no exaggeration
to say that a feeling of being members of one family prevails among
Soviet people.

(Nenarokov and Proskurin 1983: 44)

The post-1989 wave of nationalist movements revealed the falsity
of such claims – though we should not ignore the fact that ethnic
and nationalist strife was greatly reduced under communist rule.

Not only did Westerners for the most part underestimate the
potential for renewed nationalism in the Soviet Union and Eastern
Europe, they also were happy to imagine it was disappearing from
the whole world. This was a long-standing pattern. As each earlier
wave subsided, much of mainstream academic and public opinion
breathed a figurative sigh of relief and hastened to declare the
recent nationalist movements to be merely 'transitional', or at least
among the last the world would see. The model for such beliefs goes
back at least as far as Immanuel Kant's ([1804] 1970) dream of a
'perpetual peace'. The idea of growing peace is deep-rooted not
only in Enlightenment thought generally, but in social science. It
figured prominently, for example, in most of the great nineteenth-
and early twentieth-century evolutionary syntheses. Herbert
Spencer ([1853] 1974) described the master movement of modern
history as a transition from 'militant' to 'industrial' societies, and
confidently predicted that industrialized powers would seek peace
amongst themselves so as not to disturb their commercial interests.
The great French historian Elie Halévy (1930) said much the same
thing in 1930, looking back on the First World War (and not antici-
pating the second). In common with a great many analysts of the
subject, he saw violent nationalism as an exception to what should
have been the historical rule. Seen as an exceptional interruption
to the anticipated growth of world peace, nationalism was dismissed as a throwback, a matter of unfinished business, or in need
of special-case explanations in idiosyncratic historical cases.[12]

None of the other great social and political analysts has been as
widely castigated for failure to grasp the importance of nationalism
as Marx and Engels. This is so, perhaps, because Marx and Engels
were among the most overconfident of the internationalists of the
mid-nineteenth century. With the rest, they did not see clearly
enough that our very word 'international' suggests not the absence
of nations but their primacy. Still, Marx and Engels both pointed

out something crucial about nationalism even while they greatly underestimated its importance.[13] What they stressed was the ease with which ideas of national loyalty could be manipulated by elites to get working men and women to stop fighting for their rights and economic interests within their countries in order to focus on foreign threats. Their internationalism was shaped by their experience of an era in which state apparatuses admitted little popular participation, and when dissident members of a nation – like themselves – were commonly driven into exile to commune with like-minded colleagues from other nations (Kramer 1988). Marx and Engels maintained considerable German national identity, but in their writing they revealed little sense of the extent to which nationalist loyalties were heartfelt and nationalist identities basic to working people's sense of self. Accordingly, they could not anticipate nor their theories make much sense of the fact that during World War I working people would be willing to die for even extremely ambiguous 'national interests' (which national interests, moreover, were defined mainly in terms of the corporations and colonial ventures of economic elites). Equally they failed to anticipate that after communist revolutions, regimes like that of Stalin's Russia might form which not only would fail to establish the class-less society and turn the would-be worker's paradise into a hell of political repression for many, but which also would pursue great-power politics on the foundations of old empires, at once denying national autonomy to those within the borders of the Soviet Union and abandoning the vision of internationalism in favour of the interests of the Soviet state.

Above all, Marx and Engels failed to consider that few people would respond to the real material challenges of global capitalist economic integration simply as workers. In all cases, other identities were also at work. Workers suffered economic privations as heads of households, as members of communities, as religious people, as citizens – not just as workers. It was a challenge for labour activists to get working people consistently to treat their identities as workers as primary, and it was a challenge that the labour movement met with only ambiguous success. Indeed, even when they thought of themselves as members of the working class, most workers continued to think of themselves first as members of their particular craft or occupation – as printmakers, or silk weavers, or clockmakers, or longshoremen – not simply as workers.

This was especially true of skilled and relatively privileged workers who might have been best placed to lead broader working-class mobilization, but who chose as often to defend their positions against the less skilled, the more recent immigrants, and simply those not already in the union. In fact, it was only with the rise of relatively integrated states, the idea of common membership in something called the nation, and the belief that governmental legitimacy derives from the consent of the governed (all relatively modern ideas) that economic inequalities could be reflected in something like modern class differences. Marx and Engels did not give adequate recognition to the fact that these other identities – community, craft, religion, nation – not only existed but could shape the way people responded to global capitalism. They were not unique in this; most of their more academic cousins in the social sciences made the same error, and academics, politicians and journalists today continue too often to think that issues like social justice and global economic integration are somehow separate from issues like nationalist insurgency and religious fundamentalism. They are not.

2
Kinship, Ethnicity and Categorical Identities

Nationalism, we have seen, is distinctively modern. It is a way of constructing collective identities that arose alongside transformations in state power, increased long-distance economic ties, new communications and transportation capacities, and new political projects. This does not mean, however, that everything about nationalism is new. Specific nationalist identities and projects have continued to draw on ethnic identities of long standing, on local kinship and community networks, and on claimed connections to ancestral territories. This has been a crucial source of cultural content, emotional commitment, and organizational strength for such identities and projects.

It is nonetheless important analytically to distinguish nationalism from ethnicity as a way of constructing identities, and both from kinship. The distinction does not turn simply on content, since ethnicity is often presented as an extension of kinship and nationalists commonly present nations as large families sharing bonds of culture and descent. The key questions, rather, are what forms of solidarities these are and how they are reproduced. Two closely related distinctions are crucial: between networks of social relationships and categories of similar individuals, and between reproduction through directly interpersonal interactions and reproduction through the mediation of relatively impersonal agencies of large-scale cultural standardization and social organization.

Although nationalism, ethnicity and kinship represent three distinct forms of social solidarity, they may overlap – or articulate with each other – to varying degrees in specific situations. In some cases they may be mutually reinforcing; in others tensions among them may pose serious problems for attempts to forge larger 'national' solidarities in multi-ethnic societies. Focusing on the distinctions and relations among the three is important not only to grasping such specific case variations, but also to avoiding a false opposition that has characterized many analyses of nationalism. Though most good researchers are more subtle, a number of writers have been led by the force of argument to treat as mutually exclusive claims to explain nationalism by ethnicity and claims to explain it by state building and self-interested elite mobilization. They have written as though reference to pre-existing, taken-for-granted bonds must be a reference to ancient history rather than to a specific form of continuing social and cultural reproduction, and as though demonstration of invention and manipulation must somehow mean that nationalism has nothing to do with ethnicity and draws no strength from the emotional commitments people forge in their everyday social relations.

Construction vs. primordiality

One of the biggest tensions in the literature on nationalism divides 'constructivists' or 'instrumentalists' from 'primordialists'. The former emphasize the historical and sociological processes by which nations are created. Many (the 'instrumentalists') stress that this 'invention' is often a self-conscious and manipulative project carried out by elites who seek to secure their power by mobilizing followers on the basis of nationalist ideology. There is obviously much truth to the proposition that nationalist leaders often manipulate the sentiments and identities of their followers. It is also clear that nations are not eternal beings present as such from the beginning of time.

On the other hand, historical research shows noteworthy continuities between modern national cultures and their antecedents, and in patterns of geopolitical regions and relations. We can also see that nationalism derives much of its force from the phenomenological experience of ordinary people that, in general, their nations are always already there. Many of the distinguishing characteristics of national cultures, like language, are not created by individuals. Rather, individuals only become persons in social relationships that are already shaped by culture. Moreover, some of these relationships, like family and ethnic bonds, may seem so basic that people – at least in some settings – cannot imagine themselves without their attachments to these relationships.

To take such an extreme view as to deny the reality and relevance of either of these sets of observations is unreasonable. Clearly people experience their social worlds as always in some part given to them prior to their own actions. Equally clearly, many aspects of these social worlds – including the demarcation of nations – are products of human action and subject to potential manipulation. In fact, only nationalist ideologues tend to assert 'primordialist' positions so strong that they imply that nations have existed in anything close to their modern form since the beginnings of history. Social scientists studying nationalism generally recognize both (1) the role of historical change and human action, and (2) the distinction between recognizing the powerful attachments forged in people's close personal relations and early cultural experiences and determining whether and how these will translate into nationalist allegiances. Indeed, the latter is a point stressed by one of the most important of the so-called 'primordialists', the anthropologist Clifford Geertz (1963).

While most 'constructivists' or 'instrumentalists' are concerned to show that *both* nationalism and ethnicity are subject to human action and even manipulation, Geertz argues for maintaining a distinction between the two so that we can ask analytic questions about the relationship between nationalism and ethnicity. Although many later writers have stereotyped Geertz as a theorist of 'primordial nationalism', it is ethnic bonds that he treats as at least experientially primordial.[1] His main point is that in many new states (e.g. the countries created in Africa during the withdrawal of colonial powers), people's most powerful 'given' or 'taken-for-granted' attachments may be to ethnic groups such as 'tribes'.[2] These 'primordial' ties are potential threats to projects of civic nationalism and civil society.

> To an increasing degree national unity is maintained not by calls to blood and land but by a vague, intermittent, and routine allegiance to a civil state, supplemented to a greater or lesser extent by governmental use of police powers and ideological exhortation ... considered as societies, the new states are abnormally susceptible to serious disaffection based on primordial attachments ... Economic or class or intellectual disaffection threatens revolution, but disaffection based on race, language, or culture threatens partition,

irredentism, or merger, a redrawing of the very limits of the state, a
new definition of its domain.

(Geertz 1963: 110–11)

This is partly so, Geertz suggests, because these ethnic and other
'primordial' ties are of the same general order as the nation; they
are therefore more readily competing bases for constructing a new
nation or expelling members from an existing one. The nation that
is asserted as coterminous with the new state may seem a looser-
knit, emotionally thinner, and more artificial body.

The constructivist position tends, by contrast, to underestimate
the power of culture, and the force of taken-for-granted identities
that are tied to people's very practical abilities to get along in the
world. But constructivists make a crucial argument against even
subtle theories of primordial ethnic identity like Geertz's. It is rare,
they point out, to find cultures so clearly discrete, non-overlapping
and distinct that they 'automatically' become the basis for different
social groupings. Rather, as Paul Brass has argued, people's identities – even their most 'primordial' identities – are more often multiple, subject to choice, and dependent on the situation in which
they find themselves than primordialists generally recognize (1979,
1991). The very sense of being a member of a coherent and clearly
demarcated group is not simply given by tradition but raised in
certain contexts – especially when there are either tensions with
other groups or efforts by leaders to mobilize followers on the basis
of that collective identity.

One of the key points made by constructivists is that the existence of the cultural commonalities or strong affective ties to which
primordialists point does not guarantee that any particular collectivity will develop a sense of identity or mobilize for political action,
let alone claim national status. 'Given the existence in a multi-
ethnic society of an array of cultural distinctions among peoples
and of actual and potential cultural conflicts among them', Brass
asks (1979: 88–9), 'what factors are critical in determining which of
those distinctions, if any, will be used to build political identities?'
The issue is not just whether cultural commonalities exist, but how
they are constructed and reconstructed as they are called into
action by leaders and ideologues. 'The leaders of ethnic movements
invariably select from traditional cultures only those aspects that
they think will serve to unite the group and that will be useful in

promoting the interests of the group as they define them' (Brass 1979: 87).

The questions we need to ask are: (1) how does it come to be that people's experience of being at home in the world is often bound up not only with their immediate personal relations but with the larger category of the nation? (2) how can nations that are in fact historical creations come to seem 'primordial'? and (3) how do nationalist leaders and ideologues claim history and use it in mobilizing people for nationalist projects?

The invention of tradition

In an influential work, Eric Hobsbawm and Terence Ranger (1983; see also Hobsbawm 1990) have examined a number of instances in which national 'traditions' have been 'invented' by state-building elites. New states brought into existence by the withdrawal of colonial powers in Africa, for example, often produced mythological accounts of their pre-colonial roots, of the heroism of anti-colonial founders, or of the commonalities of their citizens. Not surprisingly, they played down the extent to which their borders and populations were defined arbitrarily by conflicts and compromises between colonial powers. They strove to inculcate a unifying national culture through educational programmes, state-dominated media, and the production of public ceremonies. Though commonly presented as distinctive, however, the national culture was seldom a direct extension of 'primordial' indigenous culture. It often owed a great deal to colonial powers – and to the experience of resistance to those colonial powers that helped to unite members of different tribal, ethnic, or regional groups.

This pattern does indeed seem widespread. It is particularly visible in new states, but versions of the same construction and reconstruction of common traditions have also attended nationalist transformations of older states – whether in Europe or Asia. Tennyson's account of Camelot and Scott's stories of the Highlands thus helped to invent a widely 'remembered' past for England and Scotland.[3] Communists and republican nationalists alike have engaged in a selective appropriation and reconstruction of China's past – including elements of its ancient past and accounts of more recent struggles. Indeed, Chinese educational practices make especially prominent use of exemplary narratives – whether stories of the communists' Long March or more homely tales of ordinary people who made sacrifices for their work group, their family, or their nation (Bakken 1994). Such narratives commonly carry a message about nationalist loyalty as well as other virtues. Certainly when they are exposed as myths rather than facts, this has a tendency to devalue them. Nonetheless, they form part of the broad common experience and background culture of most Chinese people.

Hobsbawm and Ranger are clearly right, then, about the invented character of much national tradition. The more dubious part of their argument is the implication that demonstrating invention invalidates traditions.[4] It is not clear why this should be so. Hobsbawm and Ranger seem to accept the notion that long-standing, 'primordial' tradition would somehow count as legitimate – the premise of nineteenth-century nationalist scholars who sought to discover which were the 'true' ethnic foundations of nationhood (see Skurnowicz (1981) on Poland and Zacek (1969) on Czechoslovakia) – and then assert by contrast that various nationalist traditions are of recent and perhaps manipulative creation. This seems doubly fallacious. First, all traditions are 'created'; none are truly primordial (as even early functionalists like Eisenstadt (1966, 1973) and Geertz (1963) acknowledged). All such creations also are potentially contested and subject to continual reshaping, whether explicit or hidden. Second, what gives tradition (or culture generally) its force is not its antiquity but its immediacy and givenness. Some nationalist self-understandings may be historically dubious yet very real as aspects of lived experience and bases for action.[5] They are taken as unconscious presuppositions by people when they consciously consider the options open to them.[6] Other claims, by contrast, may fail to persuade because they are too manifestly manipulated, or because the myth that is being proffered does not speak to the circumstances and practical commitments of the people in question. In between are claims that are accepted as part of orthodox ideology, but which people are aware may be questioned.[7] People may even join in public rituals that affirm narratives they know to be problematic, but gain an identification with these as 'our stories', a sense of collusion in the production of these fictions, and a recognition of them as background conditions of everyday life. Whether George Washington actually chopped down the cherry tree or Hafez Assad was actually the first pharmacist of Syria is not quite the point.

It is impossible to differentiate among states by showing some to be created and others not, but it is indeed possible to show that some national identities have proved more persuasive than others and more capable of becoming a part of citizens' immediate basis for action and their unquestioned (or hard to question) trans-mission of culture. It is thus not the antiquity of Eritrean national-ism that mattered in mobilizing people against Ethiopian rule, for example, but the felt reality of Eritreanness.[8]

Conversely, when circumstances and practical projects change, even seemingly settled traditions are subject to disruption and alteration. Thus Indian nationalists from the nineteenth century to Nehru were able to make a meaningful (though hardly seamless or uncontested) unity of the welter of subcontinental identities as part of their struggle against the British. The departure of the British from India changed the meaning of Congress nationalism, however, as this became the programme of an Indian state – one among several possible constructions of an Indian state – not of those outside official politics who resisted an alien regime. Among other effects of this, a rhetorical space was opened up for alternative nationalisms and 'communal' and other sectional claims that were more easily backgrounded in the colonial period (Chatterjee 1994). The opposition between primordiality and 'mere invention' leaves open a very wide range of historicities within which national and other traditions can exert real force.

Leaders who mobilize people on the basis of putatively pri-mordial ties sometimes adopt nationalist rhetoric, and sometimes try to assert definitions of nations primarily in terms of ethnic iden-tities – occasionally with disastrous, even genocidal results. Where ideas of national or ethnic identity merge with racial thinking, pri-mordialism is boosted and made especially dangerous – witness not just Germany under Hitler but Burundi and Rwanda more recently. But genocide does not automatically follow from the joining of racial thought to nationalism; it is a more complicated result of both ethnic diversity and generally state-centred political projects. Empires were generally not genocidal, as we shall consider further below; it has been states 'modernizing' with reliance on the dis-course of nationalism that have perpetrated the great examples of genocide. The impact of joining racial thinking with nationalism is not only to stigmatize 'aliens in our midst', but to reinforce national solidarity against internal cultural distinctions. This is one of the functions of the racial thinking that has been a powerful force in twentieth century China (Dittkower 1993). It has perhaps facilitated some Chinese oppression of ethnic minorities, and expansionist projects like the colonization of Tibet. But it has also and at least equally importantly encouraged the solidarity of Han Chinese against both their linguistic and regional differentiations within China and their diaspora and division into multiple states.

The notion of nation commonly involves the claim that some specific ethnic identity should be a 'trump' over all other forms of identity, including those of community, family, class, political preference, and alternative ethnic allegiances.[9] Such claims are made not just by nationalists and others engaged in ethnic politics, but implicitly by a whole range of common usages in Western history and social science – for our intellectual heritage has been shaped by nationalist ideology and the experience of nation building. Thus we habitually refer to ethnic groups, races, tribes and languages as though they were objective units, only occasionally recalling to ourselves the ambiguity of their definitions, the porousness of their boundaries, and the situational dependency of their use in practice. The point is not that such categorical identities are not real, any more than that nations are not real; it is, rather, that they are not fixed but both fluid and manipulable. Cultural and physical differences exist, but their discreteness, their identification and their invocation are all variable. Even more, the relationship of such cultural and physical differences to social groups is complex and problematic. Ethnic identity is constituted, maintained and invoked in social processes that involve diverse intentions, constructions of meaning, and conflicts (Barth 1969). Not only are there claims from competing possible collective allegiances, there are competing claims as to just what any particular ethnic or other identity means. In short, the various similarities and solidarities termed 'ethnic' may well predispose people to nationalist claims, and may even predispose others to recognize those claims, but it is difficult to see ethnicity as a 'substance' which directly gives rise to and explains nationality or nationalism.

Kinship, descent, ethnicity and nationality

Modern nations often have historical roots in old ethnic identities. But nationalism is a different way of thinking about collective identity from ethnicity, and ethnicity itself is only an aspect of the way most collective identities were organized in the past. Closely related, but more basic and pervasive, was the rhetoric of kinship and descent. It will help us to clarify the meaning of nationalism if we contrast it to these other ways of constructing connection and collective identity.

All peoples on the earth today and all known to us historically have some method of reckoning identities and connections to each other through kinship and descent.[10] They have marriages, ideas about parentage, families, and ways of determining inheritance and collective identity through either paternal lines, maternal lines, or both. But while kinship is important and family is valued in all societies, kinship and descent do not play the same role in organizing societies everywhere. In modern Western societies, for example, descent or lineage plays less of a role than it did in earlier times (when inherited aristocratic titles – and for that matter inherited rights to peasant fields – were of basic importance and when who was descended from whom might be crucial to who should marry whom), and much less of a role than it does in some other societies (such as India, where descent groups are commonly tied to certain occupations and children are expected to marry within them). Among the Tallensi of Northern Ghana, as among many of the world's 'traditional' and relatively low-technology societies, kinship and descent are (or until very recently were) the basic organizing principles for nearly all of social life (Fortes 1945, 1949; Calhoun 1980). They determine who works with whom in economic production; they guide religious practice (centred on veneration of ancestors); they provide principles for selection and respect of leaders.

The modern claim to nationhood is often evoked through the language of kinship and descent. Leaders rouse followers by calling on their loyalty to their 'brothers', and by describing the threat to the purity of the national bloodline if their sisters have children by foreigners. People speak of their nation as being like a large family, or claim blood ties, or talk of how their ancestors fought their ancient enemies in some long-ago battle.

In a crucial sense, however, it is misleading to use the language of kinship and descent to characterize nations. In contemporary Serbia, Croatia, and Bosnia, for example, kinship and family are certainly valued. They may even play a larger role in organizing social life than, say, in England, the United States, or Australia. But they are not the template of the whole social order. Orthodox Christians, Catholics, and Muslims are *not* taught to pray to their ancestors, but to God and perhaps to various saints who are not necessarily kinspeople. The office of president is not inheritable in any of the three countries. While businessmen may favour their brothers and cousins in each, their economies are organized largely on the basis of cash exchange, long-distance trade, and factories and other enterprises in which kinship is the basis of neither employment nor the organization of production.

Moreover, what is being asserted by nationalist leaders who say 'we are one family' is something very different from how family works for peoples for whom it is more basic. Serbian or Croatian leaders who say this mean that 'we' are all the same, 'we' are in this together, 'we' have an indissoluble bond, 'we' should never be divided by any loyalty to smaller or cross-cutting groups. Tallensi would recognize the moral force of such exhortations, and sometimes the members of a family might call for support from their kinsmen in similar terms. But as members of a segmentary lineage society, they would always recognize, in a way the Serb and Croat rhetoric does not, that family refers to a sliding scale of loyalties. There is the nuclear family of parents and their children, a minimal lineage linking two or more such nuclear families under a common parent (say the father of two brothers who might live in the same compound and farm together), and lineages of various inter-mediate scales all the way up to maximal lineages defined by (alleged) common ancestors as many as ten to twelve generations distant. The result is that large families are always composed of smaller families. There is no single, fixed unit so primary that a Tallensi would always think of it, rather than a larger or smaller group, as definitively his or her family (and if this is not so for descent groups, still less does it apply to the complex networks of kinship ties formed through marriages). Which level of family would matter would depend on the situation.

All Tale lineages also fit into clans, which claim common descent but are unable to trace this directly. Clans are large *categories* of more or less equivalent members, not structures of specific kin *relations*.[11] Clans do not divide into a sliding scale of clanlets as lineages naturally divide into a hierarchy of larger and smaller segments. But clans are exogamous, and so help to organize the formation of kin relations between individuals. When a man and woman marry, this forms a new web of relations between their clans, lineages, and individual family members. This provides a framework for working together when needed – whether to arrange new marriages, to trade, or to settle disputes. In sum, kinship and descent link Tallensi to each other both (1) in a dense, complex, and systematically organized network of identifiable and indeed named relationships – father/son, older brother/younger brother, etc., and (2) in a small number of categories within which people share common identities as equal members of a unitary whole, like a clan. Whenever two Tallensi meet, they can establish with great precision how they are related by intermarriage or common descent, and also where such commonalities end and they are divided by differences of descent.

An American – or a Bosnian, or a Chinese – may identify with her family, her neighbourhood, her school, her city, her state, and the country as a whole. But what is distinctive about nationalist rhetoric is that (1) it can *only* be used for the country as a whole (while the Tallensi can use kinship rhetoric to describe any level within their whole system of groups and loyalties), and (2) it presupposes that, at least in times of crisis, the claims of the whole nation have clear priority over sectional claims.[12] If segmentary kinship urges – in the words of an Arab proverb that uses more combative language than Tallensi would – 'I against my brothers, I and my brothers against our cousins, and I, my brothers, and my cousins against the world', the point of nationalism is largely to say: 'never you against your brothers, nor you and your brothers against your cousins; only the members of our national family against the world'.

Nationality, thus, becomes one large categorical identity that encompasses many smaller categories ('tribes', ethnic groups) each of which may be organized internally on the basis of further categories and complex networks of interpersonal relationships. Nationalist rhetoric posits whole categories of people without reference to their internal differentiation, or claims priority over all such internal differences; ideal-typically, one is a member of a nation directly as an individual. The rhetoric of kinship and descent constitutes society – to the extent that reference is made to such a larger whole – as a conglomeration of multiple and overlapping memberships of different segments none of which is a trump card against the others; one is a member of Tale society only through one's embeddedness in networks of kinship and descent and categories of clanship.

Ethnicity occupies something of an intermediary position between kinship and nationality. Ethnic identities have become important historically wherever multiple groups have dealings with each other in a common territory. They have developed especially where the concentration of population in a city, the development of economic links beyond the local level, and/or the creation of a state (especially an empire) has pulled distinct and internally integrated peoples into relationships with each other or with the state itself. Ethnicity is thus not simply an extension of kinship, but the way in which collective identity gets constituted when kinship loyalties, traditions, and other means of passing on common culture confront a broader arena in which most interaction is not organized by the same kinship and culture as within the group.

This happened when Tallensi moved outside their traditional area in search of jobs – and when British colonial administrators moved in. When Tallensi move to the city, they go to some lengths to maintain their kinship connections. But to non-Tallensi they are not known primarily by their families or lineages; they appear as a relatively undifferentiated group by virtue of their common cultural and behavioural characteristics and appearance. Common ancestry is assumed to account for these characteristics, but the specifics of kinship no longer matter in the same way. That is, they take on an *ethnic* identity and are known by their ethnicity. Indeed, for those migrating into cities or dealing with centralized government administrations, there are many advantages to developing a sense of ethnicity, with its potential for more general links than those provided by kinship (Horowitz 1985). But Tale ethnic identity does not reach meaningfully beyond Ghana; if Tallensi travel beyond the borders of the state, they carry passports that represent them simply as Ghanaians.

Ethnicity becomes salient at the boundary between internal ways of organizing group life (which give ethnicity most of its cultural content) and external attributions of character by others who participate in the same larger city, country, or economy. Internally, an 'ethnic group' may be organized in terms of kinship and descent or in terms of its own mix of categories and relations. Externally, vis-à-vis other ethnic groups or the state, it appears as a category of equivalently 'ethnic' members. This was as true for Jews, Greeks, Gauls, and other non-Romans under the Roman empire as for Jews, Armenian Christians, Greek Christians, and other communities under the Ottomans.[13] It was a crucial feature of 'indirect rule' in empires. Central authorities dealt with intermediary authorities, each of whom was responsible for a category of population. How the population was internally organized was of secondary (if any) concern to the centre.[14]

Ethnic identities reflect internal culture, but not in a neutral way. They reflect it along certain lines of intergroup relationships. Thus as Frederik Barth and colleagues have shown, people frequently shift their ethnic identities in order to maximize their advantage in different situations (Barth 1969; see also Horowitz 1985). Consider Kenya, where Swahili has the status of national language, but many more local languages are spoken by various ethnic groups. When members of several 'tribal' groups like Kipsigis, Kikuyu, and Maasi interact, they can choose to express their common Kenyan nationality by using Swahili – or they can express their distinct ethnicities by using their own mutually unintelligible languages. Laitin (1992) suggests that people readily manage up to three languages in such settings – a home language (sometimes only oral), a national or regional language taught at school, and an international or trading language. Where elites speak English or some other international language, groups of workers may use a local or 'pidgin' language as a way to keep bosses from understanding them and thus stress their ethnic distinction. At the same time, a worker who wants to get promoted and get ahead in the bosses' culture will try to improve his or her ability to use the international language as a way of downplaying ethnic distinction. As flexible as people are in their everyday interactions, when language becomes a matter of state policy – e.g. with regard to what is taught in schools – it can be a very hot issue. In Eritrea, for example, a proposal to teach in local mother tongues brought protests from those whose mother tongues did not have developed written literatures, especially because these groups were mainly Islamic and would have preferred instruction in Arabic. In short, it is common to be multilingual; it is not obvious where people's primary linguistic loyalties lie; and the politics of language can be much more complicated than the simple idea of respecting a 'national' language implies.

Cultural or ethnic difference is organized differently within each particular milieu. This is especially apparent where ethnicity is constructed in many different settings for a people divided by a diaspora. For example, Jews are not only ethnically diverse because of histories in disparate cultures, but which features of Jewish identity became salient – for Jews or for others – has varied enormously with context. To be Jewish thus did not mean the same thing in relation to Pharaonic Egypt as to the other peoples of what is now called Palestine, did not mean the same thing in Imperial Rome as in the Magreb, and has meant still other things in various medieval and modern European contexts and in the contemporary United States. In Germany, it meant something very different before, during, and after the Holocaust. For the Beta Israel – ethnic Jews of Northern Ethiopia, often called Falasha – to be Jewish meant something different in Ethiopia than it meant in Israel after many moved there as refugees in the 1980s.[15] While Jewish religion ostensibly unified all Israelis, the Beta Israel found that race divides Israelis. Authorities refused, for example, to mix 'black' blood with that of other Jews. Ultra-orthodox rabbis refused to recognize the Beta Israel as fully Jewish unless they went through humiliating rituals of recircumcision. And of course, even where race was not the main issue, Jews who came to Israel from different parts of the world brought a variety of influences from the settings where they and their ancestors had lived, often spoke different languages before learning Hebrew (the national language of Israel), practised different forms of Judaism, and in some cases looked different from each other.

Ethnic identities, in short, do not just come from within; they are produced in worlds of plural ethnic identities. They divide as well as unify; the boundary of the group requires internal similarity as much as external difference. In this, ethnic identities are like national identities, which also never stand alone.

Individualism and categorical identities

Nationality is only one of a number of 'categorical identities' that have assumed central importance in the modern era. These are encouraged by large scale, but they are not uniquely associated with any specific size of group. The defining characteristic is identification by similarity of attributes as a member of a set of equivalent members. Clans and age sets are both kinds of categorical identities by contrast to lineages, for example, because individuals are members of them directly rather than by mediation of webs of relationships. As we saw above, maps, with their patchwork patterns of differently coloured countries, echo the categorical identification of nations – they are containers for members who are similar insofar as national identity is definitive. This kind of categorical thinking about nations influences social scientists who take nation-states as units of analysis as though each were more or less integral and discretely bounded (see Tilly's 1984 complaint).

The discourse of nationalism thus shares much with those of race, class, gender, and other appeals to cohesion based more on the similarity of individuals than on their concrete webs of relationships. Individuals are the units that are grouped into categorical identities. Well before modern nationalism, many religious identities worked this way (Anderson 1991). A person could become a Christian, thus, by conversion, no matter who his or her relatives were, and Christians were understood to form a group – a very large group – because of their common beliefs and practices, not because of any specific kinship or other relationships among them. While Christians did have such relationships with each other, there were too many of them for this to be the primary basis of their common identity; each could have direct relationships with only a tiny part of the whole. Christians in different places varied from each other but – at least in principle – not in ways that were given theological weight. Medieval Catholicism was closer to the kinship/ethnicity model, with embeddedness in a hierarchy of parishes and authorities mattering more and individual revelation less. While their mobilization was organized on regional/political bases, the Crusades helped to foster a more categorical identity among Christians – by opposition to 'heathens', 'infidels', or Muslims.

Feudal Europe combined its own reliance on kinship and descent (not only among pretenders to the throne and aristocratic titles, but among prospective inheritors of rural property at a local level) with a hierarchy of nested categories – subjects of feudal lords at various levels from lesser lords and knights down to peasants. The hierarchy defined both occupations and social rights and responsibilities. Cities were anomalies within this conception of a 'feudal' whole, though their 'free' citizens divided into largely occupational corporations and status hierarchies. Within guilds and similar organizations, kinship might be important, but the increasingly dominant official structure of membership was categorical: there were free journeymen and employing masters.

Many in modern Europe have looked back at feudal Europe as though it were the extreme case of a traditional society, thus under-estimating both its internal dynamism and the extent to which more fully kinship- and descent-structured (and generally non-literate and non-state) societies like the Tallensi offer a sharper contrast to modern patterns.[16] As Europe modernized, it relied more and more on categorical identities. Both migration and gradual integration of regions into larger states yielded ethnic groupings. Protestantism categorized individuals as tokens of the type, 'believer'. Not coin-cidentally, categories of such believers found it easy – even com-pelling – to break apart from the larger ostensible whole. The Protestant Reformation and religious pluralism generally yielded a variety of religious categories. The emergence of a class system in place of a hierarchy of specific relationships with reciprocal obli-gations produced one of the most striking of all categorical systems – with, as Marx emphasized, proletariate and bourgeoisie alike appearing as a set of interchangeable members.[17]

While nations may have ideologies of common descent and shared kinship, they are organized primarily as categories of indi-vidual members, identified on the basis of various cultural attrib-utes – common language, religion, customs, names, etc. Nations are, moreover, commonly understood as themselves being individuals – both in the literal sense of being indivisible, and metaphorically as singular beings that move through history as ordinary people move through their biographical life courses. Yet they, too, are prone to fission. Nationalists commonly claim that the individuals of a popu-lation cannot realize their personal freedom unless the population is 'free' in the sense of political self-determination, and simul-taneously demand that the members of a putative nation adhere to some common standard of culture and behaviour.

In the main modern Western view, individuals exist in and of themselves; the basic source of identity is neither webs of relation-ships nor encompassing hierarchy (Dumont 1982; Taylor 1990; Evens 1995). This modern idea of the individual as the locus of indissoluble identity – at least potentially self-sufficient, self-contained and self-moving – is a powerful factor in nationalism. It is no accident that the modern notion of nation arises in tandem with modern ideas of the 'punctual self' or individual. The two match each other. The modern idea of the person was forged partly in the context of political philosophy and law. When Locke (1950), for example, asks under what circumstances people can be autonomous citizens, he is probing the nature of responsible personhood at the same time as he is exploring how sovereign power might be distributed among citizens. The disqualification of women and men without property is based on their being dependents, not fully autonomous. Rather than forming their own opinions as individuals, Locke thinks they will be influenced on bases other than reason by others on whom they depend for subsistence and indeed identity. Rousseau's ([1762] 1950) idea of the general will presumes a social whole, like a nation, and at the same time embodies his radical idea of the integrity and freedom – the absolute inalienability – of the individual. The general will is radically 'whole', not a matter of mere majority votes, yet it is also present in each individual member of the whole. However paradoxical it has seemed to later analysts, Rousseau captures something basic to the discourse of nationalism in asserting simultaneously the indivisibility of the individual person and of the whole community, and in claiming the possibility of an immediate relationship between the two.

The links between the histories of individualism and nationalism are perhaps most strikingly clear in the early nineteenth-century German thinker, Joachim Gottlieb Fichte. Fichte's (1968) notion of self-recognition, of the person who (as Marx caricatures it) seemingly confronts himself (or herself) in a mirror and says 'I am I', is inextricably tied to the notion of the nation as itself an individual (see also Meinecke 1970).[18] Just as persons are understood as unitary in prototypical modern thought, so are nations held to be integral. In general, each nation is understood as indivisible (literally, thus, individual) and as the bearer of a distinctive identity. Each nation had a distinct experience and character, something special to offer the world and something special to express for itself. 'Nations are individualities with particular talents and the possibilities of exploiting those talents' (Fichte, quoted in Meinecke 1970: 89). To be a 'historical nation', in Fichte's phrase, was to succeed in this process of individuation and to achieve a distinctive character, mission and destiny. Other nations lacked sufficient vigour or national character; they were destined to be failures and consigned to the backwaters of history. Marx's contemporary, Friedrich List, followed Fichte when he 'pronounced nations to be 'eternal', to constitute a unity both in space and time' (Szporluk 1988: 115). Yet List also thought that modern nations made themselves – a kind of collective *bildungsprozess* that produces true individuality out of heterogeneous constituents and influences. The nation was ideally thus a 'willed community'. All the many members of the category became one in their commitment to the whole.[19]

Individualism is important not just metaphorically, but as the basis for the central notion that individuals are directly members of the nation, that it marks each of them as having an intrinsic identity and that they commune with it immediately and as a whole. In the discourse of nationalism, one is simply Chinese, French or Eritrean. The individual does not require the mediations of family, community, region, or class to be a member of the nation. Nationality is understood precisely as an attribute of the individual, not of the intermediate associations. This way of thinking reinforces the idea of nationality as a sort of trump card in the game of identity. While it does not preclude other self-understandings, within most nationalist ideologies it is held to override them at least in times of national crisis and need. In Foucault's sense, therefore, nationality is understood as inscribed in the very body of the modern individual (Foucault 1977, 1978–88; see also Fanon 1963). A person without a country must therefore be understood to lack not only a place in the external world but a proper self (cf. Bloom 1990).

The discourse of nationalism – like those of class, race, and gender – not only encourages seeing identity as inscribed in and coterminous with the individual body; it also encourages seeing individuals as linked through their membership of a set of abstract equivalents rather than their participation in webs of concrete interpersonal relationships. It promotes categorical identities over relational ones, partly because nationalist discourse addresses large-scale collectivities in which most people could not conceivably enter into face-to-face relationships with most others.

This suggests also a different notion of moral commitment from previous modes of understanding existence. Nationalism offers the chilling potential for children to inform on their parents' infractions against the nation precisely because each individual is understood to derive his or her identity in such direct and basic ways from membership in the nation. This is sharply different from the discourse of kinship and the ideology of honour of the lineage. Their children derive their membership of the whole only through their concrete and specific relationships to parents and other kin.

Of course nationalist ideology can extol the virtues of the family and nationalist movements can be rooted in the manifold inter-personal relations of traditional society. Indeed, anti-colonial nationalists may emphasize the family and local community in order to constitute the indigenous nation outside the officially political realm dominated by the colonial state. The idea that the Chinese are not individualistic but family-oriented can be an internal claim to national distinctiveness – what 'we' Chinese are like – as well as an external attribution. Yet even in the Chinese case, with its seemingly endless discussions of 'Chineseness', pro-grammes for saving or strengthening the nation have involved a stress on forging a new kind of Chinese person. In some versions, the account of the nation continues to include strong favourable reference to family and community. These are not necessarily con-tradictory to the idea that nationalist discourse addresses a large category of equivalent individuals. Family and community can be treated rhetorically as things – or values – that all members of the nation have. Extolling them helps members to experience the whole as an extension of their more local commitments and accord-ingly to invest more wholeheartedly in it.

On the other hand, many nationalists have found the grip of tra-ditional patriarchal families and kinship groups too powerful, and sought to free individuals from their grasp both for their own benefit and so they could better serve the nation. Where the claimed priority of the nation confronted other categorical identi-ties – race, class, gender, religion – there has almost always been conflict. Each of these raises the prospect of a fundamentally divided nation in a way that predominantly relational identities like family and community need not. On the Indian subcontinent, thus, Hindu and Muslim especially, and in some places Sikh, Christian and other religions have appeared as large-scale categorical identi-ties, not just social networks. They could be invoked even by people only loosely woven into webs of interpersonal relationships with their coreligionists. The categories are often as important to South Asians living in Europe as to those at 'home', even though those living abroad may be less exclusively tied into a web of such intra-ethnic relationships. The communities coincident with these re-ligions have split the posited nation and become the basis for competing nationalisms (Jurgensmeyer 1993). The situation in Northern Ireland has some similarities. Of course, the more family and community relations are organized in accordance with divisions of categorical identities – that is, the more people marry inside categories, live only near their coreligionists, work in ethnically divided enterprises – the more category and network will coincide. This typically gives each collectivity greater capacity to mobilize for collective action. Combining category and network may not increase intergroup hostility, but it makes it easier for collectivities to act on such hostility, and reduces the chances of bringing them harmoniously together.

The transformation of ethnicity

Ethnicity is one of the possible elements that knit together a mere aggregate of persons, that make of them an identifiable – and self-identified – people. It can thus contribute powerfully to the development of a national self-consciousness and solidarity. Dense kin relations within an ethnic group can enhance social solidarity – but so can living as neighbours, joining formal organizations, and working together. Shared ethnic culture can help to provide both social solidarity and collective identity – but other forms of shared culture and political participation can also join members of different ethnic groups. Switzerland, Canada, and the United States have all developed political cultures – and consumer and media cultures – that are not reducible to the culture of any of the many ethnic groups within them. Indeed, it is one of the major hopes of many advocates of democratic political cultures that it should be possible for loyalty to constitutions or political processes and institutions to bind people together despite their ethnic differences.[20] At the same time, peoples who share a great deal of common culture and who might even be considered part of the same ethnic group – like those of Britain, New Zealand, and Australia – may nonetheless come to form different nations. Neither social solidarity nor common culture is a monopoly of ethnic groups, though ethnic groups are good at promoting both. Collective identity is not precisely equivalent to or guaranteed by common culture, though certainly it helps.

Ethnicity, in short, does not provide sociocultural groups ready to become nations. 'Nationalism is not the awakening and assertion of these mythical, supposedly natural and given units', writes

Gellner. 'It is, on the contrary, the crystallization of new units, suitable for the conditions now prevailing, though admittedly using as their raw material the cultural, historical and other inheritances from the pre-nationalist world' (Gellner 1983: 49; similar points are made by Chatterjee 1986; Hobsbawm 1990; Anderson 1991; Kedourie 1994). Breuilly (1993: 342) makes a similar point: 'the ideology is not, therefore, a gloss upon some pre-existent social reality but a constituent of that reality'.

Nationalism thus draws on previous identities and traditions, and national identities reflect those traditions. But nationalism fundamentally transforms the pre-existing ethnic identities and gives new significance to cultural inheritances. Ethnic roots and cultural distinctiveness are only aspects – and not even necessarily universal aspects – of the creation of modern nations. The United States demonstrates this well. If the citizens of the colonies that won independence from Britain in the late eighteenth century had a shared ethnicity, it was English (or perhaps British) and thus hardly was the basis for distinguishing them from Great Britain.[21] But they were also ethnically heterogeneous. Many were English, Scottish, Irish, or Welsh. Others were of Dutch or French backgrounds; some were descendants at least in part of African slaves or of Native Americans. And of course the United States has retained a national identity even while absorbing a wide range of immigrants and allowing them to retain considerable ethnic distinctiveness. Part of the key is that the United States was conceptualized – at least in part – as a willed community, which meant that membership depended on commitment, not just ethnic or other categorization. This is one of the meanings of 'civic' nationalism as distinct from ethnic. Over time, however, a new categorical identity as Americans and US citizens began to supplant the idea of willed community and to issue in arguments about essential characteristics of American culture.

It is easy to imagine that ethnic traditions are simply inherited from pre-modern life. As Anthony Smith (1986, 1991) has shown, there is a great deal of continuity in some ethnic traditions. Some peoples described in the Biblical book of Exodus still live near where they did 3000 or more years ago and have retained recognizably similar identities. But we need to be cautious on three points. First, noticing the continuity in ethnic traditions does not explain either which of these traditions last or which become the basis for nations or nationalist claims (Gellner 1983: 45). Second, traditions are not simply inherited, they have to be reproduced: stories have to be told over and again, parts of traditions have to be adapted to new circumstances to keep them meaningful, what seem like minor updatings may turn out to change meanings considerably, and the 'morals' to the stories – the lessons drawn from them – sometimes change even while the narratives stay the same. Third, the social and cultural significance of ethnic traditions is dramatically changed when they are written down, and sometimes again when they are reproduced for television and movies; in other words, ethnic traditions closely tied to the life of a small group when they are passed on by word of mouth take on a different meaning and work differently for individuals and society when they are reproduced by artistic or academic specialists, when they are enshrined in sacred texts, and when they figure in the lives of many different small groups, each with its own more local, word-of-mouth tradition.

Consider the differences between the ways traditions are woven into the nationalist stories that help to define India, and the ways very local traditions help to give identity to small communities *within* India. There are innumerable such oral traditions, centred on local temples, gods, ancestors, and events. The nationalist leader, Jawarhalal Nehru, drew on cultural traditions to write his influential nationalist history, *The Discovery of India*. But the narrative thus created and written down has both a singular authorship and a fixity that is not characteristic of India's many more local traditions. Nehru's text states a case for the whole in a rhetoric and with a content drawn partly from the partial and local traditions. But it does this interestingly in English, a common language not available to India's local traditions, and it does this in some sense against the very diversity and fluidity of local traditions. To say too simply that nationalism is grounded in ethnic traditions, thus, obscures from our view important differences in scale and mode of reproduction.

Nationalist Claims to History

Nationalism has a complex relationship to history. On the one hand, nationalism commonly encourages the production of historical accounts of the nation. Indeed, the modern discipline of history is very deeply shaped by the tradition of producing national histories designed to give readers and students a sense of their collective identity. On the other hand, however, nationalists are prone, at the very least, to the production of Whig histories, favourable accounts of 'how we came to be who we are'. A nationalist history, like Nehru's (1989) *The Discovery of India*, is a construction of the nation (and was originally published in 1949, the year of independence). The point is not just that such a history is not neutral. By its nature, nationalist historiography – that which tells the story of the nation, however accurate the facts it cites, and whether or not it is overtly bellicose or ethnocentric – embeds actors and events in the history of the nation whether or not they had any conception of that nation. *The Discovery of India* not only transforms both Dravidians and Mughals into Indians, it gives them narrative significance as actors constructing and reconstructing a common and putatively perduring phenomenon, India. Both victors and vanquished in dynastic wars and invasions become part of the story of India. Likewise, history textbooks produced in the new state of Pakistan teach schoolchildren that Pakistan can be traced back to the birth of Islam on the Arabian peninsula, and equate the spread of the Mughal empire with the history of modern Pakistan (Jalal 1995).

The same process is at work in the narratives of Western national histories. The US Civil War was a material struggle over national

unity, of course, but symbolically it has helped ever since to
constitute a common American history for descendants of those
killed on both sides of that bloody conflict (as well as for Americans whose ancestors arrived later or kept their distance). This is
one reason why the theme of fratricide is so prominent in narratives of the war. That brother fought brother helps to establish that
both sides were really members of one family (Anderson 1991:
199–201). It is no accident that the 'Pledge of Allegiance' all American schoolchildren learned for generations was created as a post-
Civil War ritual, declaring their country to be 'indivisible'.[1] The
colonial experience is taught to American schoolchildren as a
prelude to the (inevitable) formation of the USA. Native Americans and immigrants are given a clear place in nationalist recon-
structions (if not always the one they would choose). But history
writing is not only a matter of remembering everybody; it is also a
matter of erasing those divisions that are unnerving. American
textbooks still find it easier to ignore than confront the divisions of
the Vietnam War era (FitzGerald 1980; Kramer, Reid and Barney
1994). Similarly, with the end of communist regimes in the USSR
and many Eastern European countries, it has become common to
appeal to the precommunist era as a time of imagined national
unity and 'normality'. As Leszek Kolakowski (1992: 20) has
remarked: '. . . since communism was awful (as it indeed was), it will
be normal to believe that the precommunist past, czarist Russia in
particular, was an unceasing festival of hilarity. On both counts,
popular historical perception will scarcely deal with reality. There
is no point in deploring this. Self-deception is a necessary part of
life, both in the individual and in the nation; it provides us all with
moral safety'.

In the different circumstances of late-nineteenth-century France,
Ernest Renan made much the same point about the importance of
the tensions masked in nationalist invocations of history:

> Forgetting, I would even go so far as to say historical error, is a crucial
> factor in the creation of a nation, which is why progress in historical
> studies often constitutes a danger for [the principle of] nationality.
> Indeed, historical enquiry brings to light deeds of violence which took
> place at the origin of all political formations, even those whose conse-
> quences have been altogether beneficial. Unity is always effected by
> means of brutality.
>
> (Renan [1882] 1990: 11)

The 'brutality' Renan had in mind was exemplified by the St. Bartholomew's Day massacre of Huguenots, but the cultural or symbolic violence involved in forging unity could also be brutal. The eradication of once quasi-autonomous cultures, or their reduction to mere regional dialects or local customs is continually echoed in the subordination of once vital (and perhaps still important) differences in the construction of national histories. Speakers of different languages who died claiming independence are now 'remembered' as French.

Ironically, the writing of linear historical narratives of national development and the claim to primordial national identity often proceed hand in hand. Indeed, the writing of national historical narratives is so embedded in the discourse of nationalism that it almost always depends rhetorically on the presumption of some kind of pre-existing national identity in order to give the story a beginning. Anderson summarizes one English version:

> English history textbooks offer the diverting spectacle of a great Founding Father whom every schoolchild is taught to call William the Conqueror. The same child is not informed that William spoke no English, indeed could not have done so, since the English language did not exist in his epoch; nor is he or she told 'Conqueror of what?' For the only intelligible modern answer would have to be 'Conqueror of the English', which would turn the old Norman predator into a more successful precursor of Napoleon and Hitler.
>
> (Anderson 1991: 201)

Invoking national history and primordial ethnicity are both ways of responding to problems in contemporary claims to nationhood. Indian nationalists in the 1930s and 1940s, for example, were faced not only with the material problem of British colonial rule, which backed with force its denial of Indian claims to nationhood. They were faced also with difficulties in casting as a singular nation the manifest diversity of groups (including polities) on the subcontinent. Yet this is what the discourse of nationalism demanded of them. As we have seen, Nehru's *The Discovery of India* is a paradigmatic use of history writing to respond to these challenges. Nehru sought to show that India was one country against the British suggestion that without the alien Raj disunity and conflict would reign amongst its many contending peoples. Yet at almost the same time, other Indian nationalists responded to the same challenges with accounts that placed a greater stress on ethnicity. They sought to show that the unitary country, India, was essentially Hindu, not Muslim (and thus among other things was constituted 'indigenously' rather than by previous imperial invasions). Ghandi's Hindu nationalist opponent, Savarkar, was also influenced by the demands of nationalist discourse when he felt compelled to argue that 'verily the Hindus as a people differ most markedly from any other people in the world than they differ amongst themselves. All tests whatsoever of a common country, race, religion, and language that go to entitle a people to form a nation, entitle the Hindus with greater emphasis to that claim' (Savarkar 1937: 284). For a time, Nehru's side carried the day – at least among modernizers and at the level of the Indian state. But that the identity of the nation is essentially contested and not simply given by history, however ancient, is seen in the recent successes of Hindu nationalists (Jurgensmeyer 1993; van der Veer 1994; Raychaudhuri 1995).

Ethnicity as history

Most prominent twentieth-century analysts of nationalism have challenged accounts emphasizing prior ethnicity.[2] Kohn (1968) and Seton-Watson (1977) stressed the crucial role of modern politics, especially the idea of sovereignty. Hayes (1966) argued for seeing nationalism as a sort of religion. Kedourie (1994) debunked nationalism by showing the untenability of the German Romantic claims. More recently, Gellner (1983) placed emphasis on the number of cases of failed or absent nationalisms: ethnic groups which mounted either little or no attempt to become nations in the modern senses. Even if ethnicity plays a role, this suggests, it cannot be a sufficient explanation (though one imagines the nineteenth-century German Romantics would simply reply that there are strong, historic nations and weak ones destined to fade from the historic stage). Hobsbawm (1990) has largely treated nationalism as a kind of second-order political movement based on a false consciousness that ethnicity helps to produce but cannot explain because the deeper roots lie in political economy not culture. Comaroff (1991) has challenged the presumption that ethnicity exists as a phenomenon in itself, let alone as an adequate explanation of nationalism. In their different ways, all these thinkers have sought to debunk the claims to long-established ethnic identities commonly made by nationalist ideologues. They have also sought to challenge the notion that nationalism can be *explained* by pre-existing ethnicity. Most have wished to substitute an alternative master variable: industrialization, modernization, state formation, the political interests of elites, etc.

Against this backdrop, Anthony Smith (1983, 1986, 1991) has tried to show that nationalism has stronger roots in pre-modern ethnicity than others have accepted (see also Armstrong 1982 and Connor 1994). He acknowledges that nations cannot be seen as primordial or natural, but nonetheless argues that they are rooted in relatively ancient histories and in perduring ethnic consciousnesses. Smith agrees that nationalism, as ideology and movement, dates only from the later eighteenth century, but argues that the 'ethnic origins of nations' are much older. Smith focuses on *ethnie* – ethnic communities with their myths and symbols – and shows that these exist in both modern and pre-modern times, and with substantial continuity through history.

> [Because] ethnicity is largely 'mythic' and 'symbolic' in character, and because myths, symbols, memories and values are 'carried' in and by forms and genres of artifacts and activities which change only very slowly, so *ethnie*, once formed, tend to be exceptionably durable under 'normal' vicissitudes, and to persist over many generations, even centuries, forming 'moulds' within which all kinds of social and cultural processes can unfold and upon which all kinds of circumstances and pressures can exert an impact.
>
> (Smith 1986: 16)

This, he says, is the foundation both of particular nations and of the idea of nation.

Something similar had been argued by Romantic thinkers in the early nineteenth century. Particularly in Germany, language was seen as central, a link to the 'natural' origins of culture.[3] In stressing the 'originality' of the German language and the 'truly primal' nature of the German character, Fichte (1968), for example, claimed that German nationality had roots before ordinary history – though it awaited historical action (state making) to fulfil its potential.[4] Compared to the German Romantics, Smith downplays the role of language and argues that the crucial features of *ethnie* are 'folk culture', myths, historical memories, statements and terms of identity, ties to a territory and a sense of solidarity. Pre-modern *ethnie* generally lack economic unity and a clear notion of legal rights. They have widely varying relations to states. Smith (1986: 19) argues that the origins of modern nationalism lie in the successful bureaucratization of aristocratic *ethnie*, which were able to transform themselves into genuine nations only in the West. In the West, territorial centralization and consolidation went hand in hand with a growing cultural standardization. 'The indivisibility of the state entailed the cultural uniformity and homogeneity of its citizens' (1986: 134). 'It would indeed not exaggerate the matter to say that what distinguished nations from *ethnie* are in some sense, 'Western' features and qualities. Territoriality, citizenship rights, legal code and even political culture are features of society that the West has made its own. So is the realization of social mobility in a unified division of labour' (1986: 144). Well beyond the West, however, the compulsion for *ethnie* to enter the political arena is seemingly universal to the modern era. 'In order to survive, *ethnie* must take on some of the attributes of nationhood, and adopt a civic model' (1986: 157). Cross-class inclusion and mobilization for common political purposes are essential (1986: 166).

Nations, Smith suggests, are long-term processes, continually re-enacted and reconstructed; they require ethnic cores, homelands, heroes and golden ages if they are to survive. Small, breakaway nations rooted in particularist, quasi-religious visions are the most common new nationalist projects today (Smith 1986: 212–3). Nonetheless, this tendency towards the production of many new small nations is contained, Smith argues – writing before the events of 1989–92 in Eastern Europe, the Soviet Union and Africa – by the existing framework of nation states (1986: 218, 221). In sum, 'modern nations and nationalism have only extended and deepened the meanings and scope of older ethnic concepts and structures. Nationalism has certainly universalized these structures and ideals, but modern "civic" nations have not in practice really transcended ethnicity or ethnic sentiments' (1986: 216).

Smith is certainly right (except for the word 'only' in the immediately preceding quotation), though it is no more possible to explain nationalism on the basis of ethnicity alone than on the basis of state formation or any other *single* putative cause. Smith's account is more successful as a critique of the ideology of 'pure political identity'. Above all, however, what we need to see is the extent to which the discourse of nationalism itself presumes a discourse of ethnic origins. Nations cannot be explained by their 'objective' origins in *ethnie*, but some manner of reference to a putatively pre-existing people does seem to be implied or explicitly included in the vast majority of claims to national identity. America is only a partial exception, with ideas of the 'melting pot' complemented by production of a WASP (White Anglo-Saxon Protestant) ethnic identity as – at least for a long time – culturally dominant in the image of the nation.

Since independence, some Eritrean nationalists have turned for legitimacy to historical claims about the ancient distinctiveness of their country – though today's actual Eritrea is far from ethnically unified or culturally distinct from its neighbours. For 'cultural shows', the traditional dances of one of Eritrea's nine major 'peoples' – the Kunama – are brought forward as representative of the nation – partly because they are dramatic and make a good show, partly because they seem especially 'traditional', and partly because Kunama culture is wholly contained in Eritrea (though Kunama constitute only about 1 per cent of Eritreans). Highland Tigrinya culture, by contrast, is not very sharply distinct (other than in spoken language) from that of much of Ethiopia, and the roots of much lowland culture are shared with various Islamic societies around the Red Sea. Just as it was revolution not ethnicity that initially defined America, so – contrary to some nationalist discourse – the Eritrean nation was largely made in struggle against Ethiopia (not simply the pre-existing basis for that struggle). Nation making continues in state-sponsored educational, cultural, and national-service programmes. But reference to the nation as a transcendent being is also important, not least because such an idea helps to make sense of the sacrifices of fighters martyred in the struggle for independence.[5]

The rhetorical power of claims to pre-existing national identity is thus always in tension with recognition of historical processes of nation building. It is common, but not universal, for nationalist leaders to put their emphases on presumptions of primordiality. Even where such claims are influential, the meaning of ethnicity – as of nation and other claims to categorical identities – is established by means of social action, and this action is always in significant part political, even where it is not immediately about state power.

This conception moved beyond any simple notion of primordial inheritance and was distinctly a product of the Enlightenment and especially the French Revolution. As Steiner has put it:

In ways which no preceding historical phenomenon had accomplished,
the French Revolution mobilized historicity itself, seeing itself as historical, as transformative of the basic conditions of human possibility,
as invasive of the individual person.

(Steiner, 1988: 150)

This new idea of historical action was carried forward vitally in
nationalism, and in many cases coupled with a distinctive notion of
national destiny, a new teleology of history. Such conceptions were
not limited (as stereotype sometimes suggests) to German 'ethnic'
nationalism. Think of France's *mission civilisatrice*, England as the
'New Jerusalem', and ideas of 'manifest destiny' and being 'a city on
a hill' in United States history.

History, ethnicity and manipulation

Ethnic origins are a dominant theme in nationalist rhetoric. At the
same time, some nationalist discourse does focus on great acts of
founding or revolution. The emphasis is typically on the historical
novelty of the nation brought forth by the self-constituting action
of its people. Sometimes redemption of a problematic history,
rejuvenation in the face of decline, or living up to the potential of
a heroic past is also thematized. If founding has figured disproportionately in the United States, and revolution disproportionately in France, each country has also seen occasions when the
other side came to the fore. Reaganism in the United States and
Gaullism in France each promoted a nationalism more rooted in
claims to the past than to novelty. In much of Central and Eastern
Europe the rhetoric of the past is more clearly dominant (though
as we shall discuss further in the next chapter, this is not a night-
and-day contrast).

If anything, the global rhetoric of nationalism places greater
stress on the claim to a national (or at least proto-national) past,
and the first tendency of many observers uncritically shaped by
nationalist assumptions is to explain all contemporary nationalism
in terms of its ancient roots. This unfortunately discounts not only
the role nationalism has played in many struggles to found new –
and sometimes democratic – regimes, but the extent to which
nationalism is manipulated by elites in search of ideologies to
legitimate their power and mobilize potential followers. This problematic relationship between history and manipulation is nowhere

more pronounced than in the sad recent history of Bosnia-Herzegovina.

When war broke out in the former Yugoslavia, it was common
for Western observers to recall (with a shudder) that World War I
started with the assassination of the Austrian Archduke Ferdinand
in Sarajevo, that city famous today as a symbol of ethnic nationalist strife. But let us be a little clearer about what was going on (and
recognize the ambiguity in the relationship between ethnicity and
nationalism – and between either and violent conflict). The assas-
sin was not a local, but a Serb, a member of a secret society who
had come to Bosnia for the purpose. While Serbian and Croatian
nationalism had been increasingly conflictual for several decades
preceding the assassination, Bosnia-Herzegovina had been a relatively peaceful enclave of multicultural cooperation. It had only
recently been brought into the Austro-Hungarian fold, after centuries as part of the Ottoman Empire. Though ruled by Anatolian
Muslims and run largely as a military and tribute-collecting enterprise, this empire had been significantly multicultural and relatively
tolerant of ethnic and religious differences. When the Christian
rulers of Spain, Ferdinand and Isabella, expelled all Jews in 1492,
it was primarily into the Ottoman empire that they fled. Many
settled in Bosnia, where they lived mainly in peace with their
Muslim, Catholic, and Orthodox neighbours for 500 years. The
Jewish community, ironically, was one of the casualties of the fighting of the 1990s. Caught amid the violence perceived as primarily
Christian vs. Muslim, its leaders finally opted for an organized evac-
uation and removal of most of the remaining symbols of Judaism
in 1992.

For 500 years prior to the 1990s, Sarajevo had not experienced
any fighting severe enough to damage a building. Not even, as it
happens, when that young Serbian nationalist assassinated Archduke Ferdinand. Stari Most, the famous bridge at Mostar (a city
now famous for its destruction in the early 1990s), was built in 1566
by the great Ottoman leader Suleyman the Magnificent – who
enjoyed the services of a Bosnian Slavic Grand Vizier. The bridge
(before its destruction by Croatian shells in 1993) linked different
ethnic quarters of the city, and, eventually, churches could be found
standing beside mosques. The members of the different ethno-
religious groups did not simply melt into one another; they retained
their distinctiveness, but lived in peace. They competed, indeed, in

an annual diving competition in which young Muslim, Croat and Serbian men plunged from Suleyman's beautiful bridge into the Drina – a ritual at once ethnically divided and mutually engaging, a far cry from ethnic cleansing.

Prior to its fifteenth-century incorporation into the Ottoman empire, Bosnia had indeed been part of the contested frontier between Christian Europe and the expanding reach of Islam and Ottoman rule. Serbs, for example, invest a good deal of emotion in their claimed descent from the soldiers Tsar Lazar led into battle in Kosovo in 1389. These ancestors died facing almost hopeless odds rather than capitulate to the Ottomans, and veneration of their memory legitimated attacks on Bosnian Muslims 600 years later. Of course, it would be a mistake to imagine that simple memory kept this tradition alive. It had to be actively nurtured. In the 1980s and early 1990s a considerable rekindling of the fires of memory was required to make the memory of 1389 an emotionally burning issue.

Not only had there been 500 years of relative peace, but the highly localized fighting of the 1990s was different from the clashes of empires 500 to 600 years earlier. It was certainly aggravated, however, by some of the defensive manoeuvres taken by the Austro-Hungarian empire. The empire had relocated entire Serb villages into what had long been Croatian territory – precisely to take advantage of the Serbs' famous fierceness on the battlefield by making them bulwarks against possible Ottoman aggression.[6] This undercut what clarity of ethnic territory there was.

The ideology that dominated when the former Austro-Hungarian empire was carved into putative nation-states, however, asserted that national cultures historically were and should again be homogeneous and rooted in compact territories. There was an essence of Serbian identity, in other words, and one right place for Serbian people to live essentially Serb lives. This view was sharply at odds with the actual history of the region, which had rendered every country and especially every city multicultural. Nonetheless, such reasoning helped to issue in a collection of states conceived of as representing different national groups although none of them was domestically homogeneous in ethnic, linguistic or other terms. Any nationality that would truly unify the citizens of any of these states would have to be made, not simply found. But it is also true that except in temporary panics and pogroms the essentialist notion of nationality – the notion that clear and necessary criteria for inclusion can be found which are shared among all members and no non-members of the nation – was never as operative on the ground, in the making of everyday life decisions, as in the discourse of state-building and legitimacy-seeking elites. This is why inter-marriage rates between different supposedly national groups could remain quite high (30 to 40 per cent of urban marriages since World War II have been 'mixed' (Donia and Fine 1994: 9)).

Yugoslavia is sometimes conceived less as a federation that worked – though it did work to a considerable extent – than as the lid placed on a pressure-cooker of ethnic discontent. The lifting of the lid, it is imagined, simply released forces of religious and nationalist fury that had been simmering for ages. This image, unfortunately, informed both the Western media and most of the key outside actors, like the US Secretary of State, Warren Christopher (Cushman and Mestrovic 1996). In his first speech on the Bosnia war after taking office, Christopher averred that this was simply a matter of 'ancient ethnic hatreds' and there was nothing the United States or the West could do except to ameliorate the suffering through agencies like the Red Cross and limit the spread of war (or refugees).

But Christopher was wrong. He was wrong on the facts, failing to notice Bosnia's long history of peace (Donia and Fine 1994; Malcolm 1996). He was wrong to miss the role of cynical manipulation alongside sincere if extreme nationalism. He was wrong to suggest that there was nothing outsiders could do – at a time when the struggles were already being manipulated by outsiders and when the United States was supporting a discriminatory arms embargo. He was wrong to see Yugoslavia as somehow less than a 'real' nation because of its recent creation and attempt to be multi-ethnic (Denitch 1994).

While Tito's Yugoslavia was not all bad, it did help to set the stage for later nationalist conflict by drawing boundaries in such a way that the various republics of its federation would not coincide precisely with ethnic territories. As the Austro-Hungarians had done before, Yugoslavia's rulers made sure that some Serbs lived in Croatia and vice versa, this time not for military purposes but to reduce the urge to secede or to play purely ethnic politics within the federation (Banac 1984; Denitch 1994). The post-1992 attempt to make the boundaries of the breakaway states coincide with ethnic identities produced much of the fighting and human misery. The tactics of ethnic cleansing were horribly appalling. But the goal was not totally different from much nationalism throughout the world – the attempt to control a territory within which people were of a single ethnicity, spoke a single language, shared a single religion.

Contrary to Secretary Christopher's assertion that the sources of the conflict were merely ancient ethnic hatreds (an assertion with the advantage of justifying inaction), the conflict combined some rather old history with some very new features. Take the distinction between Serb and Croat. Now presented as an ancient ethnic–national distinction, as late as the early nineteenth century this was mainly a difference of religion between people who shared the same language and ethnic stock. Serbs became Orthodox under the influence of Russia, while Croats were Catholics with stronger links to the West. It was only in the nineteenth century that Serb and Croat intellectuals began to try to distinguish their languages by developing new dictionaries, new standards for correct pronunciation, and new literary styles. They did this as part of the international wave of nationalism which also brought the revitalization (if not outright reinvention) of Catalan, Gaelic, and other relatively small languages linked to separatist political ambitions elsewhere in Europe.[7]

They also did this precisely within the context of the growing crisis of the Austro-Hungarian empire and the broad realignment of geopolitical forces that brought to the fore not only a system of integrated nation-states, but modern global capitalism. The combination is what set the stage for World War I. On the one hand, capitalism had brought more and more interstate trade. On the other hand, the process of capital accumulation – of taking profits – was organized on a national basis. European states not only traded extensively with each other and throughout the world, they had drawn much of that world directly under their control through colonization. Yet internal European power relations were unstable. Domestically the years leading up to World War I were rife with labour strife, socialist agitation, and growing nationalist militancy. Internationally, the relatively stable and longer-established nation-states of the West – Britain and France especially – sought to maintain both stability and international power in the face of the efforts of Central and Eastern Europeans (including Russians) to form modern states. From a distance, the Russian empire looked much more stable than the Austrian, and West Europeans turned to Moscow for an ally against Europe's disintegrating centre. As an Austrian labour leader remarked, 'The International of the East dominated by Russia is allied with the British and French International of the West in order to deny to the middle European, middle Asiatic International access to the rest of the world and a future share in ruling the world' (Renner 1978: 124).

The international catch, of course, was that it was unclear where the proper boundaries of these developing states lay. Nationalism was rapidly replacing dynastic claims as a basis for legitimacy. But as we have seen repeatedly and traumatically throughout the twentieth century, national identity is less the pre-established answer to questions of political legitimacy than the rhetoric in which competing answers are debated. Claims to German identity, for example, could be narrower than the bounds of today's newly enlarged German state, or broad enough to include Austria and parts of Poland – not to mention Germans living as far afield as Russia and the United States.

The eventual creation of a Yugoslav state was an attempt to impose one unifying vision on the South Slavs, who indeed had long toyed with unity as a way to secure independence from Austria. It had the attraction also of securing a modicum of independence from the Russian-dominated Soviet Union. Yugoslavia – recall – was the least loyal of the East European states in its sphere of influence. Yugoslavia also performed better in economic terms than most communist states (and was more liberal politically, and more respectful of workers' rights). But it was internally rent on economic as well as ethnic and religious lines. Slovenia and Croatia were more developed economically and more integrated with the capitalist West. In addition to tourism, they traded farm goods, crafts, and some relatively small-scale manufactured goods with Italy, Austria and Germany. Serbia, by contrast, was the most Soviet-style of the republics that made up Yugoslavia. Its economic emphasis was much more on heavy industry, and much more of its trade proportionately was within the communist bloc. It was accordingly much more devastated by the collapse of communism, which deprived it of its international allies and markets, while Slovenia and Croatia only gained better access to global capitalism. This problem was aggravated by the fact that, for a long time,

Slovenia and Croatia had been taxed to subsidize the rest of Yugoslavia (including not just Serbia but the still poorer republics like Montenegro). The army, thus, was composed mainly of Serb soldiers but paid disproportionately by Slovenian and Croatian taxes. This helped to create the environment within which Slovenian and Croatian leaders were anxious to break away from Yugoslavia when the collapse of communism offered the option, and also the environment in which Germany would push for the very rapid recognition of their claims to independence and for other Westerners to agree.

Since the death of Tito in 1980, Yugoslavia had been ruled, in effect, by a committee representing different nationally defined republics, and there was no one to impose unity with any authority. Western corporations (as well as diplomats) were eager for access to the 'attractive' parts, and indifferent to the rest. Leaders in Slovenia and Croatia found receptive audiences both at home and abroad for more and more Western-sounding economic ideas (though they also promoted ethnic nationalism). Meanwhile, as communism faltered and failed to inspire much loyalty – or even acceptance – among the masses (and as the Soviet Union could afford to buy less and less of what Serbia produced), formerly communist political leaders like Slobodan Milosevic turned increasingly to using Serbian nationalism to shore up their legitimacy and power. At the same time, examples of Islamic fundamentalism abroad – and some renewed Islamic identity domestically – led to a fear that Muslim nationalism might develop in Bosnia.

After 1989, the Slovenes and Croats were embraced in the West, Yugoslavia was dismembered, and Milosevic and others were able to mobilize panic-stricken – and increasingly economically impoverished – Serbs for their message that current problems were a Western plot, their call for national defence, and their vision of a 'Greater Serbia' to include parts of Croatia and much or all of Bosnia. In some Bosnian Serb nationalists like Radovan Karodzic, they may have thought they found only puppets or allies, but they found even more virulent and radical ethnic nationalists, with less of the practical concern for economic matters.[8] Poor Bosnia also declared independence but, alone among all the former Yugoslavian republics, it embraced the model of a multi-ethnic, pluralist democracy with freedom of religion for everyone. One might have thought this would sound familiar to US leaders, and they would support the new country that chose the political system closest to their own. But, in fact, the Americans and many others found it hard to comprehend self-determination for people who did not define themselves as a mono-ethnic nation. The Western powers did not rush to recognize Bosnia-Herzegovina as they had Slovenia and Croatia. Moreover, the West had few economic interests in or ties to Bosnia – a beautiful country that had hosted a famous Olympic Games and attracted quite a few tourists, but that had little international trade. When some of the worst killing occurred between members of different ethnic groups within Bosnia, this was simply taken as proof that it wasn't a 'real' nation.

The killing was – at the outset at least – the project of those who wanted to claim large parts of Bosnia for their own different nationalist projects. But this was not evidence that Bosnia lacked justification in its claim to be a sovereign – multi-ethnic – state. It was evidence that national identity is inherently contestable – just as the precise definition of nation is essentially contested. Neither nationalist 'essence' nor national history is therefore an altogether stable basis for judgments about legitimacy and sovereignty, even if it is the modern era's predominant rhetoric for debating such claims.

State, Nation and Legitimacy

The opposition of 'state-centred' explanations for nationalism to those emphasizing prior ethnic bonds is commonly overstated. It would be a mistake to imagine that either state formation or ethnicity could provide a 'master-variable' accounting for the whole rise and character of modern nationalism. Common 'ethnic' cultures do matter in giving modern nations their identities and emotional attachments, but the creation of modern states – and the wars and other struggles between them – both transforms the way ethnicity figures in people's lives and helps determine which pre-existing cultures or ethnic groups will flourish as nations and which will fail to define politically significant identities. Such states not only shaped national identity domestically, they organized the world of interstate relations in which nationalist aspirations flourished among stateless peoples.

The rise of the modern state

The 'modernity' of the states which grew in Europe especially during and after the era of absolutist monarchies was based primarily on their enhanced administrative capacity, their unification of territories under single administrative centres, their replacement of older forms of 'indirect rule' (from tax farming to simply delegating authority to feudal nobilities) with an increasingly direct control of and intervention into their disparate territories and populations, their reliance on popular political participation, their capacity to mobilize citizens for warfare, and their assertion of clear boundaries rather than frontiers.[1] A central part of the state formation project involved the 'pacification' of life within the state's boundaries; indeed, the state's exercise of a monopoloy of violence – or at least legitimate violence – became a crucial tenet of political theory. This involved a challenge to violence by quasi-autonomous authorities, like medieval lords, as well as to brigands, highway robbers, and other outlaws. But while states sought to eliminate such pre-existing forms of non-state violence, they also created new forms and mechanisms of violence. They mobilized more and more effectively for external war, of course, but also pursued not only domestic peace but homogeneous and compliant national populations. They did so especially by the (at least putatively) legitimate force of police and other state agents. And state agents worked not only by physical force, but by means of symbolic violence. They disciplined domestic populations by means of educational systems and poor relief, religious classifications and IQ tests, criminal records and state-enforced ethnic stigmatizations. The integrated political and cultural communities we understand as nations were created in large part by the rise of such states.

Interstate conflict played an important role in changing the form and capacity of states. Military mobilization for the purpose of external warfare served both to enhance internal integration by mixing people from different regions, provinces, and socio-cultural backgrounds, and to promote nationalism through ideological indoctrination and the very processes of mobilization, combat, demobilization and return to civilian life (Hintze 1975; Tilly 1990). Not just European wars, but conflicts over colonies were important – especially in the eighteenth and nineteenth centuries. At the same time, we should not focus so much on the inter-state dimension that we forget the 'internal' processes of state formation that were linked to changes in military conflict. One of the key features of modern warfare has been increasing costs. Because of both new technology and the scale of conflicts, states had to extract unprecedented levels of resources from their societies (Brewer 1989; Mann 1993: Chapter 11). This not only required force to get civilians to part with their wealth, it encouraged rulers to support civil societies they could not fully control because these were sources of new wealth. It also led to enhanced administrative integration and capacity. Tax collection, for example, was no longer left to quasi-autonomous feudal elites or 'tax farmers', but systematized in the hands of the national government and its bureaucratic agents. As important as their material power was their knowledge of just where wealth lay.

The key is not just the identification of state with nation, thus, but the structural changes involved in the rise of the modern state. The latter made it possible to conceive of the nation as unitary. Previous political forms neither demarcated clear boundaries nor fostered internal integration and homogenization (Giddens 1984; Mann 1986). Cities dominated hinterlands; sometimes particularly powerful cities dominated networks of others together with their hinterlands. The various kinds of military (and sometimes religious) elites we call feudal controlled substantial territories but with a minimum of centralization of power and limited ability to remake everyday life. Though empires could call on subject peoples for tribute and sometimes foster substantial interaction among diverse subjects, they posed few demands for cultural homogenization.

Modern states, by contrast, policed borders, required passports, and collected customs duties. Domestically too they involved remarkable administrative integration of previously quasi-autonomous regions and localities. Not only could taxes be collected, but roads could be built, schools run, and mass communications systems created. Eventually, state power could be exercised at the farthest point of a realm as effectively as in the capital. The capacity of states to administer distant territories with growing intensity was largely due to improvements in transportation and communications infrastructure, on the one hand, and bureaucracy and related information management on the other. It was part of a general growth in large-scale social relations. More and more of social life took place through forms of mediation – markets, communications technologies, bureaucracies – which removed relationships from the realm of direct, face-to-face interaction (Deutsch 1966; Calhoun 1992).

Economic development went hand in hand with state formation in expanding this infrastructural integration of dispersed populations.[2] Long-distance trade and regional differentiation of production were factors as basic as the administration of government in the promotion of road building. The labour migrations attendant on improvements in agricultural productivity (though mostly relatively local) not only provided the workers for industrial development but unsettled stable political patterns and communal institutions for the maintenance of social order. This in turn created the occasion for much more state intervention into the daily affairs of people throughout a country. And of course the integration of economies on a national level not only knited together dispersed individuals and communities, it helped to define the unit of identity. The economy as a putatively self-regulating system of exchanges, however, did not in itself constitute the internal unity of domestic as against foreign trade. To the extent that such inner/outer distinctions operated, they were heavily dependent on states. Moreover, at the same time that exchange relations and capital accumulation were being organized at national levels they were already becoming increasingly international. International flows of goods and capital may have been dramatically accelerated in the globalization of the late twentieth century, but they are not altogether new. It is thus a mistake to think of national economies as primary; economies are not national in some autonomous way but are made so in varying degrees by state boundaries and policies, geography and physical infrastructure.

A new form of political community

The transformation and growing importance of the idea of nation was not simply a derivative result of state formation, and certainly not solely something that state makers brought about for their own convenience. On the contrary, nationalism grew partly out of popular challenges to the authority and legitimacy of those at the top of modern states. A crucial thread in the development of nationalism was the idea – and eventually the taken-for-granted, gut-level conviction – that political power could only be legitimate when it reflected the will, or at least served the interests, of the people subject to it. This locates modern nationalism in the period after the fourteenth century during which popular uprisings and political theory increasingly relied on the notion that 'the people' constituted a unified force, capable not only of rising *en masse* against an illegitimate state, but capable of bestowing legitimacy on a state that properly fitted with, and served the interests of, its people. To 'fit with' a people meant both that the boundaries of the state matched those of the nation – an important aspect of the movement towards compact and contiguous territories – and that the purposes of the state matched the interests of its citizens – conceived not only as so many individuals but as a singular nation or confederation of such nations. It also commonly meant that people and rulers should be of the same ethnic national origin (even though Englishmen imported a Dutch king in 1688, and Norwegian nationalists imported a Danish one as late as 1905). In general, as Ernest Gellner writes, nationalism has held that nations and states 'were destined for each other; that either without the other is incomplete, and constitutes a tragedy' (1983: 6).

Throughout much of European history, discussions of legitimate rule focused on arguments about divine or natural right, on questions of succession based largely on descent, and on debates about the limits which should be imposed on monarchs. When this was the case, the question of national identity either did not arise or was marginal. The identity of rulers was important, and questions might arise about a given monarch's rule over a 'people' or various 'peoples' – as when the Hapsburg royal dynasty split into branches. Calling such peoples 'nations' initially carried no particular political significance. It was simply a reference to common origins – used, for example, to distinguish groups at medieval Church conferences and universities, and as easily to distinguish students from different parts of Sweden at Uppsala University as to distinguish speakers of different vernacular languages at the University of Paris.[3] The medieval Catholic Church recognized the cultural diversity of its various 'nations' separately from the political divisions among the Christian monarchs.[4] But when questions of sovereignty began to turn on appeals to the rights, acceptance or will of 'the people', this changed. Nations then were understood as historical 'beings' possessing rights, will and the capacity to accept or refuse a particular government or even form of government.

This idea that legitimacy 'ascended' from the people had earlier roots – including in ancient Greece and Rome, and in some of the 'tribal' traditions of ancestors of modern Europeans – but it became much more pervasive in the early modern era.[5] It was also shaped decisively by the extremely broad influence of republican thought.[6] Republicanism challenged the arbitrary rights of kings in the name of the common good. The *res publica* were things that were necessarily public, shared by right. In this tradition, modern Europe saw itself as heir to the ancient Roman Republic, before Emperors subjected Rome to their arbitrary will. Republicanism turned crucially on the notion of public, and granted a powerful role to critical public discourse among members of a political community. Republicans were not necessarily democrats, though, and often saw this political community as limited to an aristocratic or commercial elite. Even self-styled democrats often retained a limited notion of the range of people who constituted the proper political community – e.g. male property-holders. The narrower public was obligated, however, to represent the interests of the broader people. Where the definition of this properly political public was initially narrow, moreover, it tended to broaden with time and attempts by various factions to secure popular support. Nationalist rhetoric both furthered and reflected this.

The new ascending account of political legitimacy was closely coupled with an increasing level of popular participation in political discourse and activity. This happened in everyday ways, as more and more people became literate and better informed about distant events (and as growing economic integration made distant events matter more clearly and immediately to them). It reached its most dramatic form, however, in revolution. In different ways, the English Civil War and the American and French Revolutions all signalled the transformation of modern politics. The capacity of 'the people' (or rather, large numbers of people acting on behalf of the whole people) to overthrow regimes was fundamentally new. Not only did these modern revolutions put new people in positions of power, they changed the very social organization of political power and the character of social life generally (Skocpol 1979).

This transformed understanding of the nature of political community and legitimacy depended in turn on the growth of ideas about non-political social organization. Whether expressed as 'nation' or 'people', reference to some recognizably bounded and internally integrated population was integral to modern notions of popular will and public opinion.[7] In other words, it was important that 'the people' be (or at least be seen as) socially integrated, not dispersed like so many grains of sand or divided into closed smaller communities and families. Politics depended in new ways on culture and society. This led political theory to depend on social theory; it was necessary to conceive of the society which a monarch ruled, not just the territory or feudatories.

An early account of social integration, parallel to the idea of nation, was offered in discussions of 'civil society'. This term, adapted in part from an image of free medieval cities, referred both to the capacity of a political community to organize itself, independent of the specific direction of state power, and to the socially organized pursuit of private ends.[8] This self-organization might be accomplished through discourse and decision making in the public sphere, or through the systemic organization of private interests in the economy. The Scottish moralists – most famously Adam Ferguson and Adam Smith – emphasized the latter in their account of early capitalist markets as arenas in which the pursuit of private ends by individual actors produced in aggregate an effective social organization not dependent on the intervention of the state. The market was thus a model for claims to the capacity for self-organization as well as the realm of specific interests to be protected from improper manipulations. Markets demonstrated, for thinkers like Ferguson and Smith, that the activities of ordinary people could regulate themselves without the intervention of government. Such claims were linked to rejections of the absolute authority of monarchs and assertions of the rights of popular sovereignty. Following Locke, these arguments placed a new emphasis on the social integration of society as such rather than merely on the aggregate of subjects. In such a view, the state no longer defined the political community directly, for its own legitimacy depended on the acquiescence or support of an already existing political community.

These new ideas about political community grew in close relationship to religion generally and the Protestant Reformation in particular. This was also a key influence on the development of the idea (and practice) of revolution in modern Europe, and had other direct influences on the development of nationalism. For one thing, the ideas of direct revelation and the importance of reading and thinking about scripture for oneself encouraged a sense of autonomy from hierarchy (which could be applied in secular as well as ecclesiastical relations). Breakaway churches often developed traditions of congregational 'self-rule', claiming the right to choose ministers as later democrats would claim the right to choose governments. The Protestant break with Church tradition also encouraged scepticism toward related claims – like the divine right of kings. Beyond this, the wars sparked by the Protestant Reformation helped to produce the alignments of political power and cultural difference that developed into national identities – Catholic France, for example, vs. Protestant England.[9] These wars also mobilized popular participation and sentiment. Reformation thought drew on the religious vocabulary of God's chosen people to sacralize the people as a body. 'The people' was seen in often coercively conformist ways as composed of those who shared specific religious revelation or understanding (nonconformers were, after all, not uncommonly burnt at the stake). This became as true of Catholic countries in the grip of counter-reformation as of Protestants pushing reform. Poland, for example, torn between the Russian Orthodox to one side and Protestant Northern Germany to the other, was deeply shaped by its Catholic religious identity – seeing itself both as a chosen people and as a martyr nation (Skurnowicz 1981). This thread of modern European nationalism drew less on ancient Rome and more on the theocratic communities led by the early Church Fathers.[10] It is thus no accident that the Puritan influence on the English Civil War offers us some of the first really modern invocations of the people as the source of legitimacy for the state. This line of development reached a peak with the French Revolution.

Just before the English Civil War, Thomas Hobbes offered a sharp and novel justification for absolute monarchy, rooted in the claim that it served the interests of the people, rather than being sanctioned only by inheritance or divine authorization (1976). *Leviathan* was a book about the commonwealth, by which Hobbes meant not only the *res publica* of Roman law but also the emerging commercial society of seventeenth-century England (see MacPherson 1976). There was no public to enjoy public goods, Hobbes argued, without the pacifying rule of a monarch. This transformed the several and separate individuals who were originally doomed to incessant war among competing private interests into a socially organized body, a people. So while monarchy served the interests of the people, the latter had no status as a society without the monarch and hence no group claims against the monarch.

Hobbes's argument transformed from within a tradition of seeing political community defined entirely by subjection to a common ruler. Instead of locating that subjection in a hierarchy of intermediate authorities (as, e.g., the inhabitants of a given region might fall into a different political community with the conquest or shifting allegiance of a superordinate nobleman), Hobbes treated each individual as directly a member of the state. The political community thus became the whole people (even if it was granted little power). This was an important step towards nationalism. During the Civil War practical politics also placed the people on the political stage: the Long Parliament is an obvious precedent, together with the active culture of broadsides and other reports on its doings – a novel idea of reporting high politics back to ordinary people (Zaret 1996). Cromwell's New Model Army – the first 'citizen army' – was at least equally important, mobilizing a broad cross-section of people in a common political as well as military enterprise.

Hobbes's arguments were challenged almost immediately by others that, despite their predominant liberalism, appear in retrospect to anticipate nineteenth-century ethnic nationalism.[11] They attempted to show the priority of political community to particular power structures. The theoretical device of social contract thinking, for example, was expanded with the idea of a 'dual contract' in which a first contract bound pre-political agents into a political community and a second bound that community (more contingently) to a ruler or a set of laws. The main initial reflection of this argument in political discourse was to locate more and more of the political initiative and basis for evaluation in the socially organized people. In the long run, such arguments were often integrated with claims to ancient, even primordial peoplehood as parts of a variety of nationalist political programmes. But 'the people' at this juncture meant mainly the politically active elites. After the Civil War, for example, John Locke (1950) published a political theory (written earlier) that appealed not only to the interests of the people as a collection of discrete individuals with different roles to play in the body politic (Hobbes's image), but to the citizenry as a body laterally connected through communication, a public. This prefigured aspects of democratic theory, but was also well suited to the context in which Locke published it: a monarchical restoration (which the English perversely call their Revolution) which in fact accorded a leading role to a revitalized, open and internally communicative aristocracy. It was arguably among this aristocracy that English nationalism had its origins, encouraging a conception of a political community strongly distinct from and able to challenge the monarch.[12]

With the rise of claims to popular sovereignty and republican rule, the notions of 'nation' and 'people' were increasingly intertwined. In the first place, claims to nationhood offered a cultural basis for the demarcation of potentially sovereign political communities.

One use of the idea of nation, in other words, was to explain which grouping of persons counted as a people – the *English* people, for example. For the idea of government in the interests of 'the people' to work, there had to be some basis for determining who was a part of the people and who was not. It was as a nation with a distinctive national identity that people could claim a right to self-determination and to government in their interests. Whenever a nation was not sovereign – when, for example, it was subject to foreign rule – this required justification of a kind that had not been necessary before. Previously, a king or emperor might rule over a variety of different culturally distinct 'peoples', and claim legitimacy based on inheritance and proper succession, possibly reinforced by the idea of divine right of kings, and commonly rooted in conquest and military power. But as the idea spread that sovereignty was rooted in the people, and that the rights of rulers were conditional on their serving the interests of the people, foreign rule became more suspect. In the eighteenth and especially the nineteenth centuries, for example, many English people would come to resent the fact that their ruling dynasty was a family of German princes (and the ruling dynasty even changed its name to the more English 'Windsor' during World War I).

The importance of this change in thinking was not readily apparent to political theorists, even ones who in other ways helped to bring it about. Locke, for example, took the existence of discrete 'peoples' more or less as a given. This led him to stretching and contortions when he tried to explain why it could sometimes be legitimate for conquered peoples to remain subject to foreign rule – and even exploitation. It did not occur to him to take the step of considering that the distinctions among peoples might be changed by their integration into a common state – even when that initially occurred by means of violence. But in fact this is often what happened.

France offers the classic example. French kings had to fight a variety of powerful regional noblemen and their followers to integrate the French state. As late as 1850, only a minority of French adults actually spoke French (Weber 1976). Yet by the twentieth century, France was one of the most culturally integrated of European countries. Educational reforms implemented in the latter part of the nineteenth century were key to the change. The new educational programme taught a common French history and a standard version of the French language, and thereby sought explicitly to increase the integration of the French nation. Likewise, violent struggles against Protestants helped to affirm the common Catholicism of France – another important aspect of its cultural unity. Not least of all, the shared participation of wide cross-sections of the French population in the Revolution and the Napoleonic Wars that followed it not only reflected but furthered its construction as a singular 'people'. So too did the annual celebrations and other collective representations by which the revolutionary tradition became a more conservative and integrating than radical and conflictual part of the national culture. In short, nation building continued after conquest, and helped to *make* the people who would constitute the basis of an increasingly democratic sovereign state.[13]

It was partly under the influence of nationalist thinking that political theorists found it hard to deal with this issue. Like Locke, most tended to take the existence of peoples – of demarcated and culturally integrated political communities – for granted in constructing their theories. They wrote as though the task for political theory was simply to formulate procedures and arrangements for the governance of such communities, not to address their constitution as particular peoples. In the great Enlightenment *Encyclopedia*, for example, Diderot saw a nation as merely 'a considerable quantity of people who inhabit a certain extent of land, closed within certain limits, and who obey the same government'.[14] Discussions of constitution in democratic theory – at least until recently – tended either to imagine a world without established communities or to imagine that the boundaries of a political community were not problematic.[15] In the real world, however, peoples were and always are constituted as such in relation to other peoples and out of the refractory stuff of pre-existing communities and conflicting claims to loyalty and peoplehood. They were, in other words, part of the complex discourse of nationalism. Democratic theory could ignore this only because it tacitly assumed what certain nationalist ideologues (like Fichte) explicitly asserted: that everyone is a member of a nation and that such nations are *the* relevant political communities. In practice, however, there is often no obvious or uncontested answer as to what the relevant political community is. Nationalism then is not the solution to the puzzle but the discourse within which struggles to settle the question are most commonly waged (too often with bullets and bombs as well as words).

A crucial dimension of nationalism, in short, is the claim that the people of a country constitute a socially integrated body, a meaningful whole. This is crucially implied, for example, in Rousseau's famous notion of the general will. The people, the nation, must be capable of a singular identity and – at least ideally – a singular voice. The nation is thus not simply a static category but a creature of common commitment to the whole and to the principles it embodies. It is as a whole that the nation is distinct from other countries, and as a whole that its members have the potential right to self-determination and a state as singular as they are. This is a two-edged sword, however, for this strong national constitution of 'the people' not only makes foreign rule appear commonly as illegitimate, but it provides the basis for the people of a country to claim that their government is illegitimate even when it is domestic. As Emile Durkheim (1950: 179–80) noted, it is not the strength of the nation-state, but usually the apparent disjunction of people and state which brings the category of nation and the phenomenon of nationalism into play.

The English Civil War was the first major European movement to evoke this dimension of nationalism. Even putting aside the powerful popular resentment of 'the Norman yoke', this was a struggle rooted in an opposition between 'the people' and 'the state'. Cromwell and the Long Parliament presented themselves as embodiments of the people even while they were engaged in state making; conversely the opposition to the crown fixed on the royal state generally, not just on the person of the king. The crucial locus was arguably not high politics but the composition of the first popular army in modern European history. The Civil War was a kind of quarrel over legitimacy far removed from previous spats over dynastic succession and even alien rule.

The French Revolution brought this idea to its apotheosis.[16] Sovereignty became an issue not merely of the state apparatus and competition over rulership, but of the people as represented in collective action. The storming of the Bastille, for example, though enacted by a comparative handful, was a symbol of the idea of the people as actor – a crucial feature of the modern notion of legitimacy. In the popular collective actions, the constitution and reconstitution of the national assembly, and the rhetoric that accompanied both, the conception of the people as an actor on the historical stage, anticipated in the English Civil War, gained clear

enough recognition to complete many modern concepts of nation
and nationalism (Kohn 1968; Steiner 1988; Hobsbawm 1990).

Article 3 of the 1789 *Declaration of the Rights of Man and Citizen*
declared: 'The principle of all sovereignty resides essentially in the
Nation. No body, no individual can exercise any authority that does
not expressly stem from the Nation' (Godechot 1964: 116). Though
the crucial term changed, the discourse of nationalism continued to
dominate the construction of the comparable article in the Constitution of 1793: 'Sovereignty resides in the people. It is one and indivisible, imprescriptible and inalienable' (Godechot 1964: 214). Such
ideas linked the revolution directly to the tradition of Rousseau and
the idea of general will ([1762] 1950). His *Considerations on the
Government of Poland* ([1771] 1962) emphasized patriotic education
capable not only of binding citizens to each other and imbuing each
with love of *la patrie*, but also of making each a distinctively national
person, giving each mind a 'national form'.[17] In the French Revolution, especially as it was interpreted on the European continent and
celebrated in successive French political struggles, the nation had
actively constituted itself as a sovereign being.

The nation as sovereign being implied an unmediated relationship between the individual member of the nation and the sovereign whole. Once such a concept of direct membership in the nation
gained primacy, it was more difficult to conceive of derogated levels
of partial or subordinate sovereignty – kings and dukes below
emperors, autonomous cities under the protection of princes, etc.
Either Burgundy was part of France or it was an alien state; if part
of France, it was merely part and not nation in itself. In the mid-
nineteenth-century United States, claims to 'states' rights' in a
weak confederacy of strong subsidiary parts were not always the
claims of several alternative nations (the Southern states) or of the
Confederacy as one alternative nation; they were often claims
against nationalism itself. Robert E. Lee might refer to Virginia as
'his country', but the 'country' to which Confederate soldiers owed
a duty was conceived from the immediate family and community
outward (and largely through a hierarchy of gentry and aristocratic
connections, not laterally). It was not conceived primarily as a categorical identity, coterminous with a single polity and culture, but
as a web of relationships to land and specific other people. Of
course, war itself reinforced the idea of the categorical commonality of Confederate citizens (as it reinforced American nationalism

for the United States as a whole). The discourse of nationalism was one of the victors in the 'war between the states'.

One catch was that appeals to this sovereign being could often be deployed as 'trump cards' against other loyalties and against critiques rooted in various internal differences among the members of the nation. Only the properly national interests could be legitimate or authoritative in the public realm; more specific identities – e.g. those of women, or workers, or members of minority religions – could at best be accepted as matters of private preference with no public standing. Too often the pressure for national unity became a pressure for conformity even in private life.[18]

To bring forward a claim on behalf of a subsidiary category of the nation – peasants, women, a racial or ethnic minority – is implicitly to challenge the presumptive goodness of the nation. It is not that nationalist ideology is intrinsically hostile to the substance of any such claims. Rather, the tension arises because of the rhetorical tendency for the demands of such subordinate groups to appear as challenges to the unity of the nation (as defined, generally, by elite groups) or to the fairness of distribution of various goods within the nation. This issue is particularly acute wherever (and to whatever extent) membership of a nation is understood in terms of ethnic homogeneity rather than adherence to common traditions of political participation that do not presume uniformity in other areas of cultural life.

Domestic integration of nations

To speak of 'self-determination' implies being able to establish what counts as a legitimate 'self', and this can never be an altogether external judgment. Nations are made by internal processes of struggle, communication, political participation, road building, education, history writing and economic development as well as by campaigns against external enemies. The struggles are not all simply over nationalism as such. Nations are built partly as a by-product of contests over economic distribution and control of the government. Nations are integrated for a variety of purposes from trade and capitalist production to state strengthening and religious zealotry. Nonetheless, nationalist ideologues and movements often mount forceful, coercive efforts to produce and ensure conformity to authoritative visions of the nation (Kedourie 1994; Keane 1995: 202).

National integration reflects underlying social structural changes, as we have seen, but it is also actively promoted, not just a functional response to changing socio-economic conditions. Ernest Gellner has argued something close to the latter position: industrial society creates nations by promoting homogenization of national culture. Gellner argues that the cultural homogeneity of modern societies is an 'essential concomitant' of industrial production with its reliance on science, technology, and mass education. 'A homogeneity imposed by objective, inescapable imperative eventually appears on the surface in the form of nationalism' (1983: 39). In other words, the nationalist drive for conformity reflects an underlying pressure from modern industry which needs this uniformity to function well. On this basis, Gellner suggests that we can ignore the creative work of the intellectuals who shaped specific nationalist doctrines: 'these thinkers did not really make much difference. . . . We seem to be in the presence of a phenomenon which springs directly and inevitably from basic changes in our shared social condition, from changes in the overall relation between society, culture and polity' (1983: 124). Such a view underestimates both the diversity of actual nationalist ideologies, and the capacity of nationalism to figure in different sorts of projects. It also implies, dubiously, that a 'post-industrial' world – or one in which fewer people were employed in heavy industry – would be a post-national world.

The idea of national identity superseded many long-standing differentiations among smaller polities, classically in Germany. Equally, it superseded the division between town and country that had been basic for most of history. Here nationalism was closely linked to capitalism. The process of creating an integrated nation-state meant converting the peasants of, say, Provence, Languedoc and Burgundy into Frenchmen. As Gellner suggests, this happened partly because industrial growth drew so many peasants into towns, and led to the construction of roads and railways joining small local markets into national ones and making possible a division of labour on a national scale. It also happened partly because of state policies – like educational standardization.

A key occasion for contact among culturally distinct members of common nations was the development of large, standing, citizen armies. These armies were an innovation of the Napoleonic Wars. Before the nineteenth century, citizen armies had been created almost exclusively in *domestic* conflicts, like the English Civil War or the American side of the Revolutionary War. International conflicts (like the British side of the American War of Independence) were fought by mercenaries, often hired in foreign lands (as the British hired Hessians to fight in America), and by troops conscripted against their will as dynastic subjects, not national citizens. These were led by aristocrats, not professional soldiers; to be an officer was a class right, not a personal accomplishment. World War I marked the last hurrah for these aristocratic officers' corps just as it marked the culmination of a process that had turned warfare into a matter of total mobilization fought by citizen armies and backed by the civilian societies' industrial production and transport systems (Dyer 1985).

National markets, improved communications (organized largely on national lines in accord with linguistic differentiations), and actual contact such as that among citizen soldiers all made different members of nation states not only more familiar with each other, but actually more *similar* to each other. This was a critical part of the process of forming integrated nations. A crucial dimension of this was the destruction of highly local crafts in favour of more nationally integrated occupational categories. The introduction of new technology and factory organization facilitated this, and indeed helped to put workers not just of different locales but of different nations in similar on-the-job circumstances. And workers were shaped not just by the technical exigencies of their work but by their participation in national culture. Indeed, part of the struggle of nineteenth- and early twentieth-century trade unions and workers' parties was not directly for economic benefits like better wages or health care, but for the right of full participation in national affairs: for eliminating property restrictions on voting, and ensuring access to free public education. As Otto Bauer remarked in 1907, foreseeing some of the forces that would lead workers to side with their nations rather than the international working class:

> Modern capitalism begins gradually to distinguish the lower classes in each nation more sharply from each other, for these classes too gain access to national education, to the cultural life of their nation, and to the national language.
>
> (Bauer [1907] 1924: 102)

In fact, it is only with the rise of relatively integrated states, the idea of common membership in something called the nation, and the belief that governmental legitimacy derives from the consent of the governed (all relatively modern ideas) that economic inequalities could be reflected in something like modern class differences.

The phenomenon of national language, as Bauer suggests, is relatively modern. Historically, of course, Latin was the main language of long-distance and cross-dynastic communication in Europe – and even that French patriot Jean d'Armagnac confessed in 1444 that he preferred to negotiate with the English in Latin because he did 'not know French well, especially to write'. As Greenfeld has remarked, the French of Paris was the *international* language of the upper classes hundreds of years before it was the national language of the common people (Greenfeld 1992: 98). In much of Eastern Europe, the nobility spoke a language peasants could not understand, and learned only a smattering of the local languages for giving household orders. It was primarily in the nineteenth century that speaking 'national' languages – like Magyar in Hungary – became a matter of self-definition for elites and encouraged a sense of commonality with the masses. It was in this same era that Eastern European scholars began to pursue linguistic standardization through philological inquiry, publication of dictionaries, and systematic orthography. They drew on German precedents and techniques. Philological inquiries are associated especially with Central Europe, where they have figured importantly in arguments about national identity. But France also lavished attention on standardization of language. Dictionaries and orthographic and grammatical reglementation were likewise prominent in the national life of England and America in the eighteenth and nineteenth centuries, as the fame of Samuel Johnson and Noah Webster attests.

Growing cultural similarity could appear in surprising dimensions of life. Take fertility as an example. Having children involves lots of culturally influenced decisions and behaviours – how early sexual relations and childbearing should begin, for example, how many children a family should have, how these should be spaced, and how important it is for a couple to wed before they conceive their first child – as opposed to before that child is born. Before the mid- to late nineteenth century, all these behaviours varied more between urban and rural areas and among counties and provinces within each European state than they did between countries. There was no distinctive pattern of national differences; even whether a country was predominantly Catholic or Protestant had no substantial statistical effect. Local conditions and local traditions were the key factors. But from the middle of the nineteenth century, in most of Europe (a little earlier in some places, a little later elsewhere) national differences began to emerge: French families began consistently to be larger than English, for example, regardless of county or province; Germans encouraged later marriage; and so forth. It is crucial to realize that the other side of international differences is domestic homogeneity. In other words, the fertility patterns of each country were becoming more uniform. National culture was superseding local variation (Watkins 1992).

In these processes, certain versions of collective culture were constructed as 'authentic', others forgotten, constructed as 'deviant', or relegated to 'minorities'. This involved not just inventing new traditions, but also the fixing of previously more flexible and continually renewed traditions and the institutionalization both of biases and of powerful agents of cultural regulation (Hobsbawm and Ranger 1983). Thus, for example, the creation of modern Turkish identity drew on precursors that could be understood as 'always already' Turkish – a mixture of Anatolian culture, Ottoman imperial heritage and Islam, but also constituting something new, something distinctively related to a non-imperial state and to the idea of nation as well as (more famously) to Western-influenced secularism. It is precisely because a nation was being forged according to standards that seemed to require internal homogeneity and authenticity that Turkish nation building was accompanied by the genocide of Armenians.

Ethnic cleansing, early and late

Recall the former Yugoslavia and the horrors of ethnic cleansing. Croats and Serbs drove each other out of their ethnically defined republics. Slovenes – equally ethnically nationalist – had few members of other ethnic groups in their territory, and so could become independent without a similarly violent drive for domestic homogeneity. In Bosnia, though, an explicitly multinational state was declared – to the anger of ethnic nationalists, especially advocates of a greater Serbia. The world was outraged at the results. As we have seen, Western leaders and news media described them as due to the peculiar ancient hatreds characteristic of the Balkan peninsula. Part of what Serbian nationalists were trying to achieve in Bosnia by rape, murder and terror, however, was precisely the uniformity of national culture that was produced over a much longer period in France.

Markets, communication and transportation infrastructures, and shared military service, are more attractive than murder and rape. But let us not think the process of national integration was all peaceful in France or other Western European countries. France is familiar as one of Europe's best integrated countries, with citizens fiercely defensive of their language and cuisine, and worried about Islamic immigrants who may dilute the national culture. Yet this homogeneity was forged not just by a highly centralized educational system but by wars of conquest in which kings – especially Bourbons – extended their rule from their base throughout what is now claimed as the 'natural' hexagon of France, eventually subduing the threats from Dukes of Normandy who were also Kings of England, and Dukes of Burgundy whose power was sometimes greater than that of France. We – along with millions of French people – recall Joan of Arc today as a paradigmatic example of a patriot, unusual because she was female, but distinguished largely because she was willing to give her life for her king and country. But Joan's death in the Hundred Years' War (1337–1453) was not part of a simple struggle between France, as we now know it, and England. It was part of a struggle for succession to the crown in which the two claimants were members of a single family, distinct largely because of a religious sacralization of the French king that was also a dimension of the French state and the cultural unification of France. And if Joan was willing to die that France might be more fully French and more purely Catholic, many of her compatriots were willing to kill for the same goal. Such conflicts only intensified. The famous 1572 St. Bartholomew's Day massacre of Huguenots was a pogrom as fierce as most in the former Soviet Union, launched against Protestants by the Valois King Charles IX and his mother – a French 'patriot' of Florentine extraction. So intense was the religious fighting that the Italian Queen Mother felt compelled to plead that this was a kind of fratricide: 'Frenchmen should not think of other Frenchmen as Turks' (Greenfeld 1992: 106). This was an early statement of the virtues of transcending religious difference in the name of national unity – but the nationalism was still ethno-cultural, not 'civic' as later revolutionaries would try to make it.

France was in part made by such religious – and partially ethnic

– 'cleansing'. As we saw in Chapter Three, by the late nineteenth century, a prominent French patriot and important theorist of nationalism, Ernst Renan ([1882] 1990), would argue that while it was academically true that such acts of violence helped to form the nation, it was important for ordinary people to forget them and take the nation as given, not violently created. We may not agree with Renan that the principle of nationality is important enough to justify such forgetting – most of us remember religious violence, pogroms, and the Holocaust itself not only to honour the dead but as cautionary tales. Renan's historical generalization seems, however, to be sound. The experience of national identity commonly depends on such forgetting.

It may be, as several theorists have argued, that the nationalism of 'late modernizers' is especially likely to turn malignant (Bendix 1964; Nairn 1977; Schwarzmantel 1991). Much of what we now think of as the peaceful patriotism of the long-established and prototypically modern Western nations is, however, the result of earlier bloody histories. The process of consolidating states and nations was long and far from automatic.[19] It was historically conflict-ridden in the states we now think of as stable democracies, just as it is conflict-ridden in emerging states. What now seem settled, almost natural national identities are the results of symbolic struggles and both cultural and very material violence. Not only violence, to be sure: national identity and common histories are also the result of cultural creativity – the writing of novels that millions want to read, the shared exposure to television programmes, common experiences like the American traumas of the Great Depression or the Kennedy assassination all join to make people feel part of a common history with each other. But when we evaluate the cultural clashes that make it hard for today's (hopefully) developing countries to move towards democratic political systems, we should remember that it is often hard to accomplish in a generation what took hundreds of years elsewhere, and the attempt to do so is especially likely to be violent.

Universalism and Parochialism

Nationalism not only comes in many forms and contexts, but carries many different political and moral values. To be a nationalist can mean to be a modernizer and unifier against putatively backward and conflict-ridden 'tribalism' or 'communalism'.[1] Or it can mean to defend chauvinistically the virtues and interests of one's own nation at the expense of others or of the common good. Nationalism gives shape to soccer loyalties and the Olympic games, as well as to wars and economic competition (Billig 1995). It may be hard to remember today, when we associate nationalism with 'backward' claims to ethnic localism, but from the 1780s to the 1870s it flourished as a liberal, cosmopolitan discourse emphasizing the freedom of all peoples. In short, the discourse of nationalism is too basic and too widespread to pigeonhole as either positive or negative. The idea of nation is so deeply embedded in modern ways of establishing both personal and collective identity that it helps people to feel located in the world, regardless of what actions they take on that sense of location.

West/East, early/late, cosmopolitan/local

Despite this, there is a strong inclination among some groups of scholars to distinguish patriotism as 'good' love of country from nationalism as a 'bad' distortion (Doob 1964; Conover and Hicks 1996). This is not only rooted in a general desire to maintain sharp distinctions between good and bad, but it reflects some of the history of nationalist discourse itself. As we saw in the previous chapter, the modern idea of nation grew up alongside the idea of democracy as part of an effort to base politics in the will of 'the people'. The nation could be identified with the people of a country against their rulers – whether these were foreigners or simply monarchs who lacked popular support. At the same time, talk of the nation could be used to mobilize the people of one country in war with their neighbours. The same appeal to Englishness, for example, could inform both the Parliamentarians who fought *against* the King and the Englishmen who fought *for* the King against the French (or at other points, against the Scots). Patriotism, thus, was a two-edged sword as far as monarchs were concerned; they had both to depend on it and worry about it. As the Austrian Emperor Francis said, when someone was recommended to him as a patriot for Austria: 'He may be a patriot for Austria, but the question is whether he is a patriot for me' (Kohn 1967: 162).

From the point of view of early liberal nationalism, such statements simply revealed what was wrong with kings and emperors. People should not be loyal to such leaders, but to their nations. It was as members of such nations that they could achieve 'self-determination', both in the sense of democratic self-rule (or at least republican constitution-making) and in the sense of autonomy from the domination of other nations. But such a liberal theory presumed that for each nation it was obvious who was an insider, a citizen, and who was an outsider, a foreigner.[2] Each person was assumed to be an internally consistent individual, and each nation was assumed to be equally internally consistent, with 'its' individuals fitting neatly and discretely within it. These individuals could thus feel justifiable pride in the achievements of their nation – and make justifiable war on its enemies – without infringing on the rights of anyone else. But this liberalism failed to deal with the reality of conflicting, overlapping, and fuzzy boundaries; it failed to address the processes by which national identities came into being and by which the populations living in any one territory were encouraged (or forced) to adopt more or less similar identities, languages, and lifestyles. The liberal theory thus took for granted the historical processes that produced relatively consensual national identities, and also typically exaggerated the extent of consensus. It labelled as 'patriotism' those cases where people with stable national identities acted with pride in their achievements or with justice against external aggression.[3] It labelled as bad 'nationalism' those other cases where people struggled with each other over the stabilization of one or another particular definition of national identity.

Not surprisingly, this view was heavily informed by an opposition between the experiences of Western and Eastern Europe. At the time when modern nationalist discourse (and modern social science) was being formed and consolidated (between the eighteenth and twentieth centuries), most Western European countries had achieved or were on the way to achieving relatively strong, stable national identities. Socio-economic integration, cultural and linguistic patterns, and political boundaries coincided to a fairly considerable extent. In Central and Eastern Europe, by contrast, there was much more conflict over what constituted a nation. German speakers were spread across some 300 states and 1500 minor principalities in 1789; and still divided into 39 more or less autonomous political units in 1815 (Mann 1993: Chapters 9, 10; 1995: 50). In political terms, at least, 'Germany' was thus more a *project* of some German speakers than an actually existing political reality. Some of these German speakers were in Austria and ruled over an empire which also included speakers of Magyar (Hungarian) and several Slavic and other languages. Many East European countries that are currently represented as independent nations in the United Nations were throughout this period subject to struggles involving not only their own members but neighbours including Russia and the Scandinavian countries. Within the borders of each country there were speakers of multiple languages and dialects, and people who supported different political visions – unity for all Slavs, for example, versus autonomy for different Slavic 'peoples'. It was in this context that 'nationalism' came to be equated with 'problems' that arose during the process of forming (or failing to form) 'normal', stable nation-states.

Poles, Magyars, Czechs, and Germans might think of their nationalist projects as basically similar to, and as just as, the patriotism of French and English. But the ideal type of relatively stable Western European countries predominated in the discourse of nationalism. Thus an opposition became common between benignly integrative 'Western' patriotism and emotionally disruptive and populist 'Eastern' nationalism (Hayes 1931, 1966; Kohn 1967, 1968; Alter 1989; Smith 1991). This West/East contrast is cognate with the opposition between 'political' or 'civic' nationalisms and 'cultural' or 'ethnic' nationalisms. In the former case, national identity is understood to be something established by legitimate membership in a constituted political state; members of the nation are understood first and foremost through their political identities as citizens. In the latter case, national identity is defined on the basis of some cultural or ethnic criteria distinct from, and arguably prior to, political citizenship.

The Germans are the most frequently cited ethnic or cultural nation. The French are the most common example of 'Western' political or civic nationalism. But though the distinction is real, it is not between two completely separate phenomena. France and Germany, and all of Western and Eastern Europe, have been shaped by the international discourse of nationalism – including both ethnic claims and civil projects of popular political participation.[4]

In eighteenth-century Europe, the two dimensions did not appear sharply distinct (Meinecke 1970; Ishay 1995). Multilinguality was one of the hallmarks of the scholar and of that novel Enlightenment creation, the intellectual. The cosmopolitan ideal of being a citizen of the world was not simply opposed to nationalism. The ideologies of nation and nationalism were born partly as ways of giving specific form and shape to citizenship in the world. This was a conception of cosmopolitan elites – who often measured their enlightenment by contrast to the rural people around them. But nationalism was a claim of 'peoples' as against dynasties, and eventually international contrasts became more powerful than rural/urban ones.

The cosmopolitan ideal came to be enshrined in a notion of nation as polity – a paradigmatically French notion – and was challenged by those who like Fichte wished to conceptualize the nation in terms of ethnicity, primordial culture or race. This is the distinction Renan ([1882] 1990) makes (in France's favour) when he distinguishes nations that are the result of the free choices of their members (a 'daily plebiscite') from those which are given an identity and cohesion independent of the voluntary will of their members. The latter sort of claim became especially common where the comparisons or competitions among putative nations were at issue, rather than between nations and dynastic rulers. Even primordial versions of nationalism, however, invoked an element of universalism in claiming to be of the form 'nation' even when they counterpoised particular nations to other universalist discourses.

With the spreading critique of absolute monarchy and the rise of republican ideology, concern for the definition of the political community grew rapidly. The citizen of the world had also to be a citizen of somewhere in particular. This was a continuing focus of social contract theory, and with Rousseau a much stronger notion of community was added to arguments about the choices of free individuals. Rousseau was also deeply interested in the origins and impact of language as the basis for that community, and an advocate (in *Emile*) of better teaching of the 'natural' language. In general, however, late eighteenth-century France did not focus the attention on language that became characteristic of Germany. There was growing demand for the use of vernacular French (instead of Latin and Greek), and some push towards linguistic standardization (though, as we have noted, this process was far from complete in the mid-nineteenth century). But the French did not rush to equate French nationality with speaking French. Not only did various local dialects remain strong, the eighteenth- and nineteenth-century *College de France* did not even have a professorship of French language.[5] French ideas about citizenship remained overwhelmingly political rather than ethnic (Kohn 1968; Brubaker 1992; Kedourie 1994). On this basis, France provided the dominant modern story of successful formation of a nation-state. Over an extended period of time, disparate duchies and other feudal territories were transformed into provinces of the new nation-state and knitted into an increasingly effective centralized power structure concentrated in a primate city. State action in education, transportation, and other arenas promoted economic and cultural integration.[6]

To the east, the process of state formation worked out somewhat differently. Where a central French state had pursued national integration for centuries, only late in the nineteenth century did German state builders achieve any substantial political unification of the culturally similar German peoples, and only briefly under the Third Reich did this unification reach nearly completely throughout German Europe. An intense and ethnically-oriented German nationalism was nurtured by the state builders – famously between the eras of Bismarck and Hitler. This was not just a domestic development, however, but grew in a world in which nationalism was a shared way of understanding political boundaries and claims to legitimacy. The very power of this international discourse was part of the impetus for the intense struggle of many Germans to establish a strong sense of national identity. Without a unified German state, they felt, the virtues of German culture would be less appreciated and the German people would not be treated with comparable respect to others whose political lives were already organized on the model of the nation-state.

In this context, language and other ethnic criteria gained enormous importance in the definition of German nationality and the struggle for unification. Where Rousseau had sought the process by which natural autonomy was transmuted into national societies and subjected to corrupting sovereignty, the German Romantics argued that every person belonged by nature to an ideally sovereign nation. Despite political fragmentation, the German language was spoken with more commonality throughout the German states than was French in politically centralized France. In the writings of scholars like Herder, Schleiermacher, and Fichte, language was described as the distinctive expression of a particular form of life, developed by it to enable its unique experience and contribution to history. Original, primitive languages were held to be superior, thus, to composite, derived languages because they directly reflected the spirit of the people who spoke them. Borrowings were corruptions. Language, thus, was the key test of the existence of a nation (Kedourie 1994: 62–73). It was joined, moreover, with ideas of race, culture and in general ethnicity to signal that the nation was primordial and membership in it immutable.[7]

The contrast between France and Germany has been enduring. France has been much more willing to grant immigrants French citizenship, while Germany – equally open to immigration in numerical terms – generally refuses its immigrants German citizenship unless they are already ethnic Germans (Brubaker 1992). We should not take the contrast too far, however. Anxiety over language as a basis for national identity seems today more acute in France than Germany. As Smith (1986: 149) has remarked, 'all nations bear the impress of both territorial and ethnic principles and components, and represent an uneasy confluence of a more recent "civic" and a more ancient "genealogical" model of social cultural organization'. The ethnic conception of *la patrie* stood behind the late nineteenth-century anti-Semitic attack on Dreyfus; Maurras sought to define a true French nation free of Jews, Protestants, Freemasons and other foreigners (Sutton 1982). This heritage remains important in debates over immigration (Todorov 1990;

Noiriel 1991, 1996). In 1991, as protests and debates over immigration rattled French politics, conservative former President Giscard d'Estaing made a surprisingly 'ethnicist' assertion about the true French identity, apparently seeking to curry favour with anti-immigrant voters. He was rebuked not only by the left, but also by the conservative former prime minister and leader of the *Rassemblement pour la Republique*, Jacques Chirac: 'I believe that law of common descent, *stricto sensu*, or a law essentially of blood, does not conform . . . either to the republican tradition or to the historical tradition of France'.[8]

The local amid the global

The discourse of nationalism developed partly in an effort to conceptualize identities on a scale and in a form commensurate to the development of modern capitalist markets and modern states with their intense administrative capacity and ability to mobilize citizens in war. The organizing capacity of individuals' direct social relationships – e.g. family, community – was rendered inadequate by large-scale, seemingly distant structures of indirect relations (Calhoun 1991, 1992). The idea of nation – and action based on this idea – responded to this dramatic expansion in the scale on which social life is organized. The making of modern maps, as described earlier, exemplifies this.

Local relations remain important to people; communities are still often vital. But these local relationships are not capable of organizing the large-scale activities wrought by the formation of modern states and capitalism. New identities and movements arise, not just in response to but on the basis of the new scale of social organization and cultural transmission. Thus contemporary Islamic movements are products of economic, political, and cultural globalization, not simply local reactions.[9] Not only do they knit together various predominantly Islamic countries, they are nurtured in part by the experience of life in Islamic enclaves within parts of the West. Thus the message of the Ayatollah Khomeini was honed in French exile as well as in the holy city of Qom; his messages spread more widely through the world by tape recordings than the *Communist Manifesto* ever did in Marx's lifetime or than the 'modernist' arguments of 'Young Europe' or 'Young Turkey'. They found, for example, receptive audiences in South Asian Muslim enclaves in Britain as well as in Islamic countries from Sudan to Pakistan. The message was perhaps reactionary in relation to much of the modern West and to the forms Westernization had taken in Iran and the rest of the Islamic world. But it was also universalizing and in some ways cosmopolitan *within* the Islamic world. It addressed Muslims as individuals wherever they might be, and as members of the great community of Islamic faith, but not primarily as members of intermediate ethnicities or local polities. The ideology of Islamic fundamentalism is not liberal but in many variants it is universalizing. It is an international, indeed global, way of conceptualizing the local.

While nations can be integrated by dense networks of social relations and institutional interdependence, their very scale means that they are first and foremost categorical identities. No matter how well-integrated they are in terms of culture or social institutions, they cannot possibly be tight-knit personal networks. While nationalist ideologies may rely on a rhetoric of 'community' and 'family', nations are importantly distinct from such necessarily more local groupings rooted in directly interpersonal relationships.

The idea of nation is also inherently international and works partly by contraposition of different nations to each other. Nationalist rhetoric offers a way of conceptualizing the identity of any one country that presumes the existence of other more or less comparable units. Prior to the rise of nationalism, many varieties of social groupings and polities coexisted, without having need to debate or claim equivalence – city-states, principalities, tribes, kingdoms, etc. The world could in principle have one or five empires; they could relate directly to each other or to less encompassing polities. Internally, different kinds of political units may report to an imperial centre – kings and dukes, tribal chiefs and local military strongmen may all bring tribute without any standardization. The Chinese empire is a good example of one that recognized a variety of kinds of internal constituents and external tributaries. There was a fundamental transformation when, largely under the impetus of European expansion, Chinese people began to reconceptualize their country as a nation, one among many approximate equivalents.

Conceptualizing China – or any other putative nation-state – as one unit in a world-system of such states, reflected not only globalization, but a change in the meaning of the 'local'. On the one hand, the nation-state was itself made the bearer of local identity in international contexts. On the other hand, the realms of directly interpersonal relationships and smaller-scale communities, ethnicities, and regional groupings were constituted as 'interior' to the nation-state. They became its internal affairs: for example, China claims the right to be free from external intervention in its handling of Tibet – which it claims is only a locality within China, not a nation in its own right. The rhetoric of nationalism presented nations as mediators between the global (the world system of nation-states and transnational organizations) and the local (the internal affairs and internal lines of cultural or other distinction). The nation might include local (sub-national) variations, but it had to claim an overarching commonality or unity among them in order to present itself internationally as the singular bearer of local identity. This alone gave it the rhetorical claim to a singular selfhood, for purposes of self-determination, and on this basis a singular state. One result of this was to make ethnic and other groups that crossed national boundaries – like the Kurds divided among Turkey, Iraq, and Iran – into anomalies. In a nationalist world, the only proper way to be local was to be contained within a nation.

To use the international rhetoric of nationalism to claim local self-determination was not only to commit oneself to representing local distinctiveness in internationally recognizable terms. It was also to make the local nation a token of a global type, to construct it as equivalent to other nations. We can see the ironies of this change of perspective in the case of reconstructing ancient China as a modern nation. This reconstruction was not simply an imposition of the international rhetoric; it was the product of a Chinese discourse that combined older indigenous roots with the predominantly Western rhetoric of national identity, giving the latter its own distinctive inflections.

In the late nineteenth and early twentieth centuries, the idea of nation was a distinctively new way for the Chinese to understand what it meant to be Chinese. China had been understood previously – for millennia – as a 'world', or as the 'middle kingdom' that occupied the heart and vast majority of that world. This conception did not recognize a larger world within which China was only one of many equivalent units. It constituted China not as a state, or as a civilization, but as civilization itself.

This 'culturalist' understanding of large-scale collective identity contrasted sharply with nationalist thought. In the older view, Chinese culture was a singular whole, to which individuals and particular generations might conform better or worse, might measure up more or less well. This is part of what helped to define the famous 'generalist' learning of the literati-officials of Confucian China: 'his learning was not just valuable for office [or for vocational tasks], but happened to be *the* body of learning, artistic as well as moral, which was valuable in itself' (Levenson 1958: 42). Where in the older mode of thinking, any innovation had to be justified by demonstration that it was in accord with tradition, in the new approach both innovations and traditional inheritances alike required justification by demonstration that they served the interests of the nation.

One of the key steps in this change was constituting China as one of a number of like units undergoing 'parallel histories'.[10] Instead of describing China as a world or as a civilization, intellectuals at the end of the nineteenth century and especially the beginning of the twentieth began to adopt the word *guo* which had previously been used to indicate a kingdom. Within imperial China, there could be a number of such kingdoms; Confucian China could even recognize the existence of barbarian kingdoms in this sense, like tribute-paying Korea. But after the turn of the century, China itself began to be described more and more often as a *guo*. At first this was sometimes still linked to dynasty; the *guo* meant literally the object of a particular ruling regime, as in *Qingguo*, which reduced the imperial regime to the status of merely one ruling power (Levenson 1958: 98–114; Dittmer and Kim 1993). In early usage, *guo* was identified with nobility, who might fall into one or another such large unit, not with ordinary people who were beneath this kind of political identity. Gradually, however, the meaning began to shift towards the notion of people; China became *Zhongguo* or in a compound, *Zhongguoren*, the Chinese nation.[11]

Where a *guo* had formerly been a political unit, defined only by its power, it became now a repository of ultimate values. But unlike the notion of Chinese or Confucian civilization, which had constituted *the* good, the *guo* was a being capable of benefiting from a variety of goods. It was valued, but it also experienced the value of various specific goods, from wealth to military power (Schwartz 1964). With this redefinition, China could both retain its specific cultural content, and adopt a formal constitution as one of the world's many sovereign nations. A resolution could be offered to the nagging problem of to what extent China could learn from the West without forfeiting her essence. The answer was a variant of the old 'Ti-Yong' instruction to rely on Chinese learning for spiritual essence, and Western learning only for practical purposes. But now practical purposes could take more of an upper hand; instrumental criteria could be employed to justify Chinese learning; and lessons could be drawn on any of the many matters in which China was comparable as a nation to the other nations of the world. These possible lessons were among the topics most actively debated in the new periodical press that sprang up in China in the early twentieth century (Chow 1960; Schwarcz 1986; Huang 1996). In China as elsewhere, the rise of literacy and print culture both enabled explorations of international cultural resources and facilitated the creation of a relatively large-scale domestic public sphere (which was itself crucial to the emergence of nationalist thought).

Nonetheless, too much assimilation of foreign ideas could make even modernizers nervous. In 1934, the *Guomindang* (or Chinese Nationalist Party) wrote in a handbook that:

> A nation must always remain faithful to its own history and its own culture in order to maintain an independent existence on earth. For a people to keep faith with itself and progress courageously, it ought not to renounce its own old civilization lest it become like a river without a source or a tree without roots. While wishing to assimilate the new knowledge of western civilization, we ought to give it for a base the principles of Confucius. The whole people must learn the doctrine and conform to the thoughts of Confucius.
>
> (Levenson 1958: 106)

But though this was a way of talking about being distinctively Chinese, it was a way of doing so that cast this as the specifically local content of one token of a universal type, nation. Indeed, in the pursuit of nation-state development – progress – an entire literature developed of 'historical warnings from perished countries' (see Hunt 1993 on the historical writings of Yu Danchu). Marxism similarly was simultaneously both a Western import that came with certain understandings of 'nations' and stages of history, and an ideology that could be appropriated and remade in the service of largely nationalist Chinese visions and ambitions (Hoston 1994).

This kind of discourse shaped the construction of national identities, not only in China but throughout the world, where claims to distinctive local identities – to be Chinese, or Turkish, or Spanish – were usually couched in terms shaped crucially by the cosmopolitan discourse of nationalism. Nationalism was always a discourse about the multiplicity and distinctiveness of nations, of course, but it was also about the constitution of nations as the agents of history by whose interests progress might be assessed. This figured sharply in the late nineteenth- and early twentieth-century production of nations in place both of empires and of disunified principalities.

Not all states were in comparable positions to exercise central power, and not all could claim to have integrated 'their nation' within their borders. China was (and is) remarkable for the extent of cultural unity obtaining among a very large population.[12] But Chinese national identity was also both ascribed to and chosen by millions of Chinese residing outside the borders of China, people also marked by varying degrees of assimilation to other collective identities – in the Philippines, Hawaii, Indonesia, Malaysia and elsewhere. Many of the principal backers of the Republican Revolution of 1911 were precisely these ambiguous partial outsiders; many others were students returned from study abroad. Both those groups certainly had grounds for the claim to be Chinese; they were also both different from the prototypical and putatively maximally authentic Chinese constructed in literature and nationalist discourse.

The existence of members of the culturally defined Chinese nation lying outside the politically defined Chinese state has been a thorn in the side of Chinese rulers – and other Chinese nationalists – throughout the modern era. They chafed especially when parts of Chinese territory (together with populations of Chinese people) were claimed by European powers or Japan, but also over divisions among ethnic Chinese with divergent political regimes. 'Irredentism', or the attempt to restore unified rule to a larger, ostensibly national, territory is thus deeply ingrained in Chinese political thought.

The 1997 'reunification' of Hong Kong with the People's Republic of China (PRC) (together with the return of Macao by Portugal) marks an end to the purely colonial version of this problem. Note, however, the way in which the people of Hong Kong are defined as merely a local variant within the Chinese nation – to be handed back by Imperial Britain – and thus precisely not as a 'self' deserving of self-determination. And note how the PRC becomes the representative of the Chinese nation – so that transferring Hong Kong to the state power of the PRC is conceptualized as a 'return' even though the PRC was not created until more than 100 years after Hong Kong became a British colony. The idea of nation defined in terms of prepolitical cultural unity 'trumped' the notion of democratic self-determination.

Whether the same will happen in the case of the Republic of China (Taiwan) remains to be seen. Certainly Taiwan is constituted much more substantially than Hong Kong as an autonomous state. But its Guomindang ruling elites (immigrants from the mainland) have drawn sustenance from the same ideology of national unity as their communist counterparts in the PRC. They have contended that there is a single Chinese nation, which in principle should have a single state, but which is temporarily disunified by unfortunate historical accident. Efforts to rethink this are hotly contested by some within Taiwan as well as by the PRC.

Ethnic and other diversity within the nation has been a relatively modest issue in China, though it is a growing concern. It is raised not only by the handover of Hong Kong, but by the intransigence of the Chinese government in the face of rebellions among ethnic minorities like the Uiger in Xinjiang Province, and by peoples like the Tibetans who have a national identity and aspirations of their own and are harder to class as simply a domestic ethnic minority. Yet even as it comes to the fore in China, it pales as an issue by comparison to other former empires like the Austro-Hungarian whose nationalist-fuelled collapse helped precipitate World War I, and the Soviet Union, whose collapse has fuelled so many of today's nationalist conflicts.

Are some nations more 'real' than others?

As we saw in the introduction, no definition of nation has ever achieved general acceptance (Smith 1973, 1983; Seton-Watson 1977; Alter 1989; Connor 1994). This reflects the deep embeddedness of the discourse of nationalism in the practical problems of modern politics. The ideas of nation, nationality and the like are 'essentially contested' because any particular definition of them will privilege some collectivities, interests and identities and damage the claims of others (on 'essentially contested concepts' see Gallie 1967; Connolly 1974). Consider, for example, the idea that, by definition, a nation should be big enough to be autonomous and self-sustaining. Who is to say just what scale is required? Is Lichtenstein not a nation? Palau? Stalin used this argument against the claims of various 'nationalities' in the Soviet Union. Some of these now dominate states recognized by the United Nations. And in the modern global economy (and international defence linkages), what nation-state is completely autonomous and self-sustaining? Does Norway count as a nation even though small only because North Sea oil makes it rich? Will Eritrea (with about the same population) count only if it too finds oil? There is no objective way to determine which nations are 'real' on the basis of potential for political or economic autonomy.

Nationhood, thus, cannot be defined objectively, prior to political processes, on either cultural or social structural grounds. This is so, crucially, because nations are in part made by nationalism. They exist only when their members understand themselves through the discursive framework of national identity, and they are commonly forged in the struggle carried out by some members of the nation-in-the-making to get others to recognize its genuine nation-ness and grant it autonomy or other rights. The crucial thing to grasp here is that nations exist only within the context of nationalism. 'Nation', is a particular way of thinking about what it means to be a people, and how the people thus defined might fit into a broader world-system. The nationalist way of thinking and speaking helps to make nations. There is no objective way to determine what is a nation. There are no indicators that are adequate independent of the claims made on behalf of putative nations, and the political processes by which they are made good or fail to be made good. Of course, this has not stopped many political actors and some social scientists from trying to come up with objective indicators of 'full' or 'real' or 'historical' nations.

Extensive debates have focused on the distinction between 'nation' and 'nationality'. Stalin, among others, approached this as though it could be an objective question. He put forward the notion that national rights should be granted only if a people shared a common character, language, territory, economic organization, and psychic formation (Stalin 1976). Full nations shared these characteristics, and the nation thus constituted a totality. Mere nationalities shared only some of these characteristics. Another Marxist writer, the Austrian Otto Bauer, emphasized the notion of 'common destiny'. 'The nation is the totality of men bound together through a common destiny into a community of character . . . The *totality* of the associated characters . . . distinguished them from the narrower communities of character within the nation, which never create a natural and cultural community that is determined by its own destiny, but only one that is closely connected with the whole nation, and consequently determined by the destiny of the latter' (Bauer [1907] 1924: 107). But as the stress on totality makes clear, the distinction of nations from less total groups is inescapably political. The stakes are entitlement to self-determination vs. consignment to be a constituent group in some other nation.

The distinction grew up within the contexts of various empires. Even while imperial rule was still recognized, some peoples – nations – were recognized as cohesive units. Within the Austro-Hungarian empire, thus, both Austrians and Hungarians were defined as nations, even though neither Austria nor Hungary was strictly an autonomous state. Both were entitled to have direct relations, as totalities, with the emperor. But gypsies and Jews were only nationalities, groups with ethnic identity but no entitlement to even a subordinate state. They did not have comparable collective claims, according to the nationalist ideology common to elites in that setting. Slovenes, Poles, Slovaks, Czechs and the like occupied an intermediate position.

Similarly, in the former Soviet Union, a number of 'nations' were recognized as the basis of different allegedly autonomous republics – Ukrainians and Armenians, for example. Other groups, like Chechens, Tatars, and Jews were recognized only as 'nationalities', which meant that they might be counted together in censuses, and have some special political status or entitlement to special treatment, but they were not granted even nominally autonomous political space. They were seen as necessarily either spread in small minorities through the lands of real nations or as interstitial groups intrinsically dependent on those around them.

The distinction between nation and nationality is not of much help in social science, but it has had considerable appeal to ideologists involved in the processes of nation building and sorting out the claims to various levels of self-determination brought forward by diverse peoples within former empires. Thus, for example, the former Ethiopian empire was culturally and ethnically extremely diverse. The dominant ethnic group, the Amhara (not unlike the

Russians in both the Tsarist empire and its successor, the Soviet Union), pursued a programme of imposing aspects of their culture on other peoples within their empire. Protecting and extending Ethiopian national identity by means of Amharicization was an old policy, pursued with considerable force from the late nineteenth century. It gained momentum under the rule of Emperor Haile Selassie, though in conceptualizing himself as emperor he recognized not only the appeal of old traditional titles, but the ethnic diversity in his realm and the quasi-feudal system of semi-autonomous regions and a hierarchy of nobility and lordship. Under the communist government that replaced Emperor Haile Selassie, the conception that Ethiopia was in fact a single nation, though ethnically diverse, was if anything promulgated with more energy – and with direr penalties for disagreement. The government fought hard against those who claimed autonomy for nations that it regarded as mere constituent nationalities. Eritreans succeeded in claiming independence on the ground of being a true nation, fighting a lengthy civil war to make good that claim. Oromo, by contrast, remain subject to rule from Addis Ababa (though Ethiopia's 1993 constitution grants considerable autonomy to the newly demarcated 'Oromia'). Some ideologists present this as theoretically justified on the grounds that Oromo constitute a mere 'nationality' while Ethiopia and Eritrea are real nations.

In fact, it is no paradox to say that the Eritrean nation was *made* largely through its very struggle for independence.[13] But the issue is not only one of military success. During its 30 years of struggle, Eritrea became more socially integrated (for example as members of different religions and ethnic groups fought side by side and formed personal relationships), developed a stronger collective identity – and one that was inscribed deeper into individual Eritreans' self-consciousness – and spread much more widely a clear conception of Eritreanness based on the rhetoric of nationalism. It is entirely possible that the Oromo people will yet prove – and forge – their nationhood through struggles of their own. As Karl Deutsch (1966: 105) remarked, 'nationalities turn into nations when they acquire power to back up their aspirations'.

Anti-colonial and anti-imperial nationalisms depend on the internal organizing capacity of the would-be independent nation. They cannot be understood as attempts simply to protect or restore traditional arrangements, even where that is their manifest ideological purpose, for they pursue a new, national form of mobilization as a more or less necessary concomitant of anti-imperial struggle. Such anti-colonial movements also often rebel against domestic elites who have entered into accommodationist agreements with imperial powers (as was the case in Korea's March 30 movement and China's May 4 movement, both of 1919).

In both Korea and China, nationalist discourse remained extremely state-centred despite movements that attacked both traditional elites and imperial powers. There were only halting efforts in each case to develop national integration outside the purview of state power. In India, these efforts went much further. Indian nationalists brought forward in both ideology and practice a nation that was defined in social relational and cultural terms as against the political terms monopolized by the colonial state (Chatterjee 1994). In different but comparably dramatic ways in all three cases, the extent of material (social relational, economic, infrastructural) as well as cultural national integration was insufficient to sustain completely the integrity of the nation after the departure of imperial powers and/or the collapse of accommodationist domestic regimes. The partition of India and Pakistan (and the later independence of Bangladesh as well as communal separatism in India), the division of the two Koreas and the warlords era in China all suggest the limits to the national integration that could be accomplished in opposition to the prevailing state power. In each case, one of the key challenges the post-independence states took on was to resume the struggle for national integration, equating the nation now increasingly with the state.

If one major source of nationalism is new levels of national integration, it is also true that secessionist nationalisms are often forged from failed projects of broader national integration. Several East European countries and the former Soviet Union offer ample examples (Chirot 1991). The post-colonial states are particularly vulnerable to challenges from subordinate national groups, since these can employ the very rhetoric that the anti-colonialists used in winning their independence struggles. This is why the discourse of nationalism encompasses both fissiparous or secessionist movements and unificationist or 'pan-'nationalist movements (Snyder 1982, 1984; Alter 1989; Smith 1991). Croatian or Ukrainian nationalism and pan-Slavic nationalism arise from the same discursive formation. Neither secessionist nationalisms from India to

Ethiopia nor attempts to reunite divided nations from Germany through Yemen or Korea can claim clear precedence. Efforts to forge a more unified national state often inspire contrary efforts on the part of subordinate groups or neighbours. The formation of a larger unity is accompanied by rearrangements of national identities that create new lines of tension while overcoming some established ones. Thus programmes for the unification of Europe draw on new histories that emphasize the commonality of the European experience and identity; the specificity of Europe is counterposed to the rest of the world, rather than the specificity of France being counterposed to Britain or the Netherlands. At the same time, fringe nationalist movements (and claims for regional autonomy) flourish within the European Community (Tiryakian and Rogowski 1985; Delanty 1995; Kupchan 1995; Brubaker 1996; Guibernau 1996).

The discourse of nationalism can be employed equally in the service of unification or secession. Its focus is generally on the matching of a state to a putatively pre-existing nation; the scope of the national unit is not determined by the *form* of the nationalist discourse. It is a content given, in large part, by the relationship of national integration, cultural tradition and contraposition to other states within the world system. To emphasize any one of these to the exclusion of the others would be an error.

Imperialism, Colonialism and the World-System of Nation-States

Imperial rule is precisely *not* the attempt to forge a unity between nation and state.[1] In the late nineteenth-century Austro-Hungarian Empire, for example, though some of their advisers encouraged the idea, the Hapsburgs did not attempt to integrate their dominions into a modern nation-state. That is, they did not begin to treat their subjects as more or less interchangeable members of the polity, impose linguistic uniformity, build an infrastructure rendering communication and commerce easy throughout the realm, replace narratives of conquest with those of primordial ethnic commonality, or base claims to legitimacy on the interests or will of 'the people'. Imperial rule, as they approached it, left local and ethnic groups largely intact. When such empires declined, these local groups continued to exist, and sometimes gained or regained significant autonomy. Only in the modern era, however, has the rhetoric of nationalism been employed to recast these local and ethnic groups as nations.

In the territories of the declining Austro-Hungarian Empire, nationalist discourse was widely invoked against the old imperial state. This reflected both prior cultural differences and – arguably more importantly – the way in which the Hapsburgs themselves had divided their dominions into administrative units.[2] But nationalism

– in the sense of either identity or movement – did not spring spontaneously from either sort of precondition; it was given shape by the active intervention of cultural producers and political leaders. In the Austro-Hungarian case and in general, it is a mistake to characterize these emerging nationalist elites as 'traditional leaders'. On the contrary, the nationalists were largely members of subordinated ethnic or regional groups who had been educated in the imperial capital, employed in the imperial bureaucracy, or otherwise significantly involved with the imperial system. This gave them both a broader view of the situation of their 'homelands' or 'peoples' and access to the international discourse of nationalism. Often, slights to their pride or limits to their careers within the imperial apparatus gave them an incentive to focus more on nationalist projects. While such leaders – like the rest of us – were commonly motivated by selfish interests, these were not only political interests. Much of the work of creating national identity was undertaken by artists, musicians, writers and intellectuals. These did not seek political power so much as cultural distinction – and a cultural field within which to enjoy it. Other elites were, of course, more directly interested in attaining power in newly independent national states. They found nationalist rhetoric both an effective tool for mobilization and a ready framework for claiming international recognition.

Anderson has seen one of the key roots to the entire discourse of nationalism in the frustrations and solidarities of an earlier group of colonial elites (1991: Chapter 4). The Hispanic colonization of Latin America produced a peculiar career pattern that resulted in early nationalist challenges to established authorities. Spanish America was divided into a variety of administrative units. The very top officials of these were customarily sent out from Spain (and might aspire to return to higher level positions at home). Under them, however, served a large body of creole officials. These were Spaniards by descent, language and (for the most part) culture. But they were locally born. They generally could not aspire to 'return' to Spain. Their careers thus reached a barrier above which they could not go; this served to remind them of their difference – however culturally minute – from the 'true' Spaniards above them. Even more importantly, their careers were laterally circumscribed. While someone sent out from Spain might move from one colony to another, the creoles could only hold positions within the colony into which they were born – Mexico, say, or Chile. This encouraged an identification with that administrative unit as a kind of homeland. So did the fact that unlike landlords (feudal or otherwise) who generally remained in one place, tied to their locality and their land, these creole colonial officials moved from place to place around the colony. The leaders among them wound up in its capital, no matter where they were born, but usually after seeing more of the country than members of other elite groups. As educated elites, these colonial officials were also especially likely to be able to participate in the print communications that eventually provided the cultural basis for national unification.

All these factors lay behind the fact that some of the earliest clearly nationalist revolutions in the world were led by people who were privileged elites, who spoke the same language, and who shared the same religion with those whose rule they challenged. In Anderson's view, it was not in the imperial metropole but in the colonies that people first came to conceptualize themselves as bearers of distinctive nationalities rather than simply subjects of monarchs, speakers of languages, etc. Once its development began, however, the notion of nation entered into cosmopolitan discourse, ultimately informing European thought and radical politics of the eighteenth and nineteenth centuries, and anti-colonial nationalism throughout the world.

The Hispanic case of a creole elite was relatively unusual, but it was common for nationalism to be borne by elites who at once remained privileged under colonial rule but who found their aspirations blocked. In most of the world, when new elites were created, they consisted of indigenous people who received colonial and even metropolitan educations (Markakis 1987; Brass 1991; Davidson 1992). These new elites had varying relationships with more established ones. In the British Sudan, for example, they were sharply distinct in the nineteenth century when a charismatic traditionalist, the Mahdi, led a great rebellion. By the twentieth century, however, his descendant Sadiq el-Mahdi, a future Islamist prime minister, was educated at Oxford. His family had joined with many in the middle classes in a complex mixture of colonial education and anti-colonial sentiment. Colonialism rendered traditional hereditary elites subalterns even where they retained many privileges, and it blocked the upward mobility possible on the basis of metropolitan or metropolitan-style educations and similar meritocratic recruitment mechanisms. These elites among the colonized often found their best political strategy to lie in embracing the idea of nation. This meant identifying with their countrymen of all classes, despite the frequent irony of continued pride in both traditional status and new educations. They might privately disdain the non-elite among their countrymen, but publicly they sought to represent peasants and others as a singular nation oppressed by the imperial power and deserving of self-determination. This strategy worked better to the extent that the elites forged actual ties to peasants and other non-elites, and were genuinely moved by feelings of solidarity with them. Sadiq's embrace of increasingly 'fundamentalist' Islam was linked to his pursuit of such ties.

These elites did not have to invent the discourse of nationalism from scratch. As Anderson has argued, it was 'modular', and could be transplanted from one setting to another. Indeed, it may be more precise to say that the discourse of nationalism was available as an international discourse, and new groups of people could take it up, could participate in it, and could in varying degrees innovate with it. Thus when traditional elites who were displaced by colonial powers drew on the discourse of nationalism to frame their opposition to colonial rule, they combined indigenous traditions and international rhetoric in ways that could be strikingly innovative and which could transform both indigenous and international ideas. It was, for example, under the influence of the rhetoric of nationalism that indigenous elites in India, China, Ghana and Indonesia all took up the notion that legitimacy should depend on the will of those governed. This marked a change (of varying degree) in local discourses of legitimacy. At the same time, in each setting the anti-colonial elites made something different of the nationalism they drew from international discourse. They innovated, they drew in different local features, and they contended in each setting with each other on what mix of local tradition, international discourse and innovation was right.[3]

The metaphor of 'modularity' is thus potentially misleading. It suggests that elements of an international discourse can be transplanted without basic alteration to new cultural settings. This neglects the more complex interplay between each local culture and the international discourse (as well as the lines of tension within each local cultural field).[4] It also neglects the fact that developments of anti-colonial nationalism were shaped not just by discourse, ideology, and tradition, but by power relations and social structure. Specific nationalist ideologies were (and are) developed in the context of struggles and practical activity, not altogether in the abstract. It would be a mistake to imagine that every nationalist movement invented nationalism anew, entirely out of its local cultural and political resources. Equally, though, in stressing the international dimension of nationalist discourse, we must avoid the implication that later nationalisms are simply derivative of earlier ones, rather than rooted in local conditions and experience (Chatterjee 1986). That the discursive form of nationalism is internationally available does not suggest that each use of it is necessarily derivative, with the pejorative connotation of that word, any more than each successive use of the literary form of the novel must be considered derivative.

Colonialism drove nationalism forward even while it resisted it. In most settings, the presence and power of the colonial regime stimulated the affirmation or development of a national identity as counterweight and basis for resistance. In many cases, colonial ideology also stimulated nationalism by claiming that the colonized were essentially disunited (except for the peace maintained by the colonizers) and incapable of self-organization; nationalism was both the visible evidence against this and in some cases part of the actual achievement of capacity for self-organization on a large scale.[5]

Colonial rule was itself more sharply incapacitating, in a crucial sense, once the world was organized in a system of states. Regardless of the difficulties in achieving either international efficacy or domestic self-organization, both opportunities were effectively limited to those who could mount a successful claim to state sovereignty. Whatever the actual form of government claimants anticipated, no matter how elite the anti-colonialists and how elitist their agendas for post-colonial rule, their claims to sovereignty came by definition from 'below', from 'the people', rather than from the rulers above. Nationalism was (and remains) the most readily available discursive form for such claims. Though it is in part imported from an international discourse, the very colonial situation leads to its indigenous reinvention and reinforcement.

A central theme of anti-colonial nationalism is the production of a citizenry. This helps to explain why so much of the early activity of nationalists is focused not directly on contesting state power but on efforts to reform culture, to undo traditional family forms and communal loyalties, and to create a 'new person' combining aspects of Western individualism with distinctively indigenous cultural content. In attempting to account for the strength of imperial powers while demonstrating the continuing importance of indigenous national culture, many anti-colonial nationalisms produce or reproduce a split between spiritual and material life. The material realm is that in which the military and technical strength of foreign powers is evident. The spiritual realm is that in which the moral and cultural strengths of the subject nation can be celebrated. This resulted, in China, in the famous 'Ti-Yong' dictum: Chinese studies for spiritual essence; Western studies for practical use (Chow 1960; Spence 1990). In India too, nationalist ideology declared the 'domain of the spiritual its sovereign territory' and sought to restrict colonial interventions into this realm (Chatterjee 1994: 5).

> In fact, as Indian nationalists in the late nineteenth century argued, not only was it undesirable to imitate the West in anything other than the material aspects of life, it was even unnecessary to do so, because in the spiritual domain the East was superior to the West. What was necessary was to cultivate the material techniques of modern Western civilization while retaining and strengthening the distinctive spiritual essence of the national culture.
>
> (Chatterjee 1994: 133)

This rationale for selective Westernization continues to operate as part of the programme of nationalist modernization in India and China today, despite other dramatic changes in each country. It shapes, for example, Deng Xiaoping's promotion of some capitalist economic reforms while simultaneously condemning the spiritual pollution brought by Westernization.

Indian intellectuals from the nineteenth century onwards were commonly at least as cosmopolitan as Europeans. But cosmospolitanism was problematic in the context of colonial rule in a way it was not for the European enlighteners. Many Indian nationalists (including Nehru) wrote in English and spoke it more comfortably than any 'Indian' language; they helped, indeed, to make English an Indian language. But this involved a tension between English as the language of the colonizer and as the putative *lingua franca* that was to help constitute one nation by cutting across the linguistic divisions of the subcontinent. Moreover, at the same time that some nationalists appropriated English as an Indian language, others produced a renaissance of modern Indian languages like Bengali and Marathi; nationalism meant producing a new, modern literature in the vernacular languages. This shaped the attempt to forge a unity between the language of literature and intellectuals and that of ordinary people – since groups previously separated by a linguistic hierarchy were now to be united by *national* language. Chinese intellectuals pursued a similar goal in the early twentieth century – and it shaped the practices of the communist party as well.

Though much of this is distinctively a response to colonialism, Western history also involved struggles over cultural identity and the constitution of a citizenry.[6] Even Hobbes's justification of the absolute sovereignty of kings, as we saw, required first a body of citizens – a nation – capable of granting the right to rule in explicit or implicit social contract. These citizens were, perforce, not only basically interchangeable as members of the nation (i.e. individuals) but engaged with each other in common projects mediated by webs of communication.

This is a crucial contrast between the empire and the nation-state, or, as Weintraub has noted, between the cosmopolitan city and the polis. The creation of a political community called for a new kind of interrelationship, and something more than a 'live and let live' urbanity. In the cosmopolis or empire, since 'heterogeneous multitudes were not called upon to be citizens, they could remain in apolitical coexistence, and each could do as he wished without the occasion to deliberate with his neighbors' (Weintraub 1997). In both the polis and the modern nation-state, membership in a common polity requires more than tolerance and common subjection to an external sovereign. It requires mutual communication.

Modern states developed as the primary arenas for popular political participation (and in some cases the creation of democratic institutions). Indeed, it was precisely because modern states were based on citizens not subjects that their cultural politics were so violent. Historical empires were relatively effective at enabling people of different ethnic groups to live together in peace. In and around the Ottoman capital of Istanbul, for example, Jews, Christians, and Muslims lived and traded with each other. But peace was relatively easy because the different groups were not called upon to join in common deliberations about government or public affairs; the Sultan consulted advisers of various ethnic groups, but not the ordinary people. While members of various groups might be conscripted into his armies, these were not citizen armies and there was no mass mobilization for military efforts. Likewise, while the Ottoman empire (like other empires) maintained the peace vital to long-distance trade, it did not in itself produce a real economic integration among its diverse territories. It did not transform the division of labour, for example, or generate a great deal of technical innovation. This meant that most of the different communities and peoples under Ottoman rule continued to pursue their traditional and mainly local economic activities. Metropolitan merchants traded over long distances mainly in luxury goods. Otherwise, the various countries remained more or less self-contained local economies. Even within a country like Britain, this was the case until the era of the industrial revolution (including the explosion of agricultural and craft productivity that immediately preceded factory production). There was some regional division of labour based on differences in mineral endowment, agricultural potential of the land, and local craft specializations. But markets meant physical places to which local people went to trade mainly with other local people; only certain relatively specialized goods were manufactured for national consumption.

The development of institutions and arenas for sharing in popular politics ironically has often led to ideologies demanding increased homogeneity among citizens. Differences that did not matter much when ordinary people were not empowered to make political decisions became troubling with greater democracy. Enhanced national communications media – important to democracy – also can facilitate erasure of differences among citizens. One of the crucial questions of the modern era is whether meaningful, politically efficacious public discourse can be achieved without this erasure (Eley 1992; Fraser 1992). The differences which nationalist discourse commonly subjugates include gender and class as well as region, ancestry and other possible bases of counter-nationalist secession.

Though nationalist self-descriptions generally emphasize mass participation and cross-class unity, for example, nationalism is often an elite project structured in ways which maintain or institute patterns of domination. This is nowhere more true than in those post-colonial states where it is most vociferously denied. As Markakis remarks, 'anti-colonial nationalism was not, as often depicted, a massive popular crusade driven by the desire to undo what imperialism had wrought. In fact, its constituency was socially circumscribed and its aims concrete' (Markakis 1987: 70). Nationalism was commonly a project of groups linked to the colonial state and to vested interests in the colonial economy. Indeed, nationalism often grew earliest among those educated (or at least experienced) in imperial metropoles. Yet, since anti-colonial nationalists challenged the legitimacy of colonial rule on the grounds that it did not represent the indigenous people (as a general category, not just the elites among them), they helped pave the rhetorical foundations for more popular claims to political participation and restructuring. At the same time, the social relations elites forged outside their own ranks, and the 'modernizing' educational and social reform projects they undertook among 'the masses', often led precisely to a 'de-massification' of ordinary people. Where colonialists claimed that their power was necessary to keep the peace and secure economic progress, indigenous elites sought to create or demonstrate the existence of an indigenous nation adequate to the modern era (Davidson 1992). In doing so, they provided ordinary people with increased means of mobilizing for their own projects in competition with those of the initial nationalist elites. In a host of settings, for example, class-based claims could be supported by nationalists primarily when they were directed against colonial or international imperialists. They became more problematic after independence.

Claims on behalf of women have often been particularly problematic for anti-colonial nationalist groups for two reasons. First, Western colonial powers often seized on the 'traditional' treatment of women as evidence of the inherently oppressive nature of the entire cultural tradition of the colonized (and thus of the virtues of colonial rule as modernization). Raising women's issues was easily made to look anti-nationalist. Second, the effort to defend the 'spiritual essence' of the nation often involved emphasizing the national identity found in social life outside the realms of economy and public administration. Home, family and gender relations were particularly national (and attempts to introduce new forms of employment for women and other putative 'freedoms' appeared as encroachments). Wearing of the veil in Algeria thus became a complex focus of colonial tensions with France. As Fanon (1965: 65, original italics) put it, 'The veil was worn because tradition demanded a rigid separation of the sexes, but also because the occupier *was bent on unveiling Algeria.*' The colonists presented themselves as modernizers and liberators of women by challenging the veil; many Algerians understood this not only as an attack on male privilege but as an attack on traditional culture, female modesty and virtue, and Islam itself.

> The dominant administration . . . described the immense possibilities of woman, unfortunately transformed by the Algerian man into an inert, demonetized, indeed, dehumanized object. The behavior of the Algerian was very firmly denounced and described as medieval and barbaric . . . Around the family life of the Algerian, the occupier piled up a whole mass of judgments, appraisals, reasons, accumulated anecdotes and edifying examples, thus attempting to confine the Algerian within a circle of guilt.
>
> (Fanon 1965: 38)

Fanon's analysis of this tension is perhaps insufficiently critical of the patriarchal dimension of the veil – including claims that Algerian women needed its 'protection and reassurance' – but it sheds light on 'the new dialectic of the body and the world' (1965: 59) that developed when the freedom or 'protection' and 'disciplining' of female bodies became a site of contestation between Algerian nationalists and French modernizers who were also colonialists.[7] As Fanon notes, women entering the liberation struggle gave up the veil almost as commonly as those entering French-dominated social life. But there was a 'dynamism of the veil' that was missed by those who saw it as a pure embodiment of patriarchal tradition, who missed the ways in which it could be used for more political ends. This sheds some light on the more recent struggles over the wearing of the veil by Islamic schoolgirls in France itself. Regardless of the merits of the arguments over secularism vs. religious identities, it needs to be grasped that the state is not neutral but an agent of French nationalism, and that it addresses an issue with a history in colonialism and anti-colonial struggle. More generally, it suggests reasons beyond simple patriarchy for the tendency of nationalist movements so commonly to affirm masculinist practices rooted in traditional cultures (see also Chatterjee 1994).

Even beyond these specific contexts, nationalisms have been overwhelmingly male ideologies, not simply in the sense that men have been more nationalist than women, but rather in the way that national strength is defined so often as international potency and military power; men are treated as potential martyrs while women are mainly their mothers. It is in content – militarism and the appropriation of patriarchal traditional culture, for the most part – that nationalisms are especially sexist. In form, nationalist appeals to the equivalence of individual members of the nation offer a potential basis for women to claim greater rights (as indeed they have done within many polities, and by no means only in the West). At the same time, however, nationalist rhetoric has commonly embodied an emphasis on procreation, thinking of the nation's future in the reproduction or growth of its population. This is one of the reasons why rape was so significantly a crime of Serbian nationalists defiling those they wished to drive from the territory they claimed in Bosnia. This heterosexism also links nationalism in many settings both to repression of homosexuality and a normalization of sex as the basis of childbearing – on behalf of the nation.

One of the ways in which nationalisms can appear as 'modernizing' is that they promote an element of individualism (potentially though not necessarily linked to the notion that individuals are the bearers of rights) – even while they may repress strong individual differences. Thus Indian nationalism, for example, has attempted not only to create a historical narrative of Indian unity, but to address individuals directly as Indians rather than first and foremost as members of different linguistic or regional groups, castes, etc.[8] In China too, communist ideology has been essentially nationalist (even more than that of the *Guomindang*) in demanding the direct and unmediated allegiance of each individual and challenging the independent claims of parents over children (most notoriously in the Cultural Revolution). As noted above, contemporary Islamic nationalism, however 'fundamentalist' and 'traditional' in content, shares a good deal of the same discursive form. It works as a categorical identity that posits a direct connection between the individual Muslim and both the specific Islamic nation and the Umma Islam. This is part of what makes fundamentalist Islam so threatening to various formally more traditional governments like the monarchies of the Gulf states. These Arab states are precisely *not* nationalist and not organized around modern ideas of citizenship. Kuwait is ruled by an Emir, head of a royal lineage within a tribal kin group that comprises a minority of the inhabitants of its territory and an even smaller percentage of those involved in material production or rendering services. Both Iraq's Baathist nationalism and the broader Islamic nationalism promulgated by Iran start from the premise of universal citizenship, at least for men. Both officially empower individuals through elections, something Kuwait emphatically does not do. Fundamentalist Islam (and cognate nationalisms) offers an ideology much closer, in this respect, to that of the French Revolution than purveyors of common stereotypes like to admit (drawing as they do on oppositions of the Western Enlightenment to both fundamentalist religion in general and the Islamic East in particular). Nationalist discourse, in each case, commonly involves a demand for conformity not just an offer of membership. It has been potentially oppressive for all those placed in subordinate positions by the ideal-typical representation of the nation. But it has helped make individual citizens.

Capitalism and large-scale societal integration

The creation of the world-system of states was intimately linked to the expansion of capitalism (Wallerstein 1974–88). The state was not only a facilitator of this expansion, it was a response to it (Anderson 1974; Kennedy 1987). Both efforts to participate in the global market and efforts to opt out in favour of autarky required strong states. States mediated activity in the global market system (and shaped the process of capital accumulation), even though from very early on this global market transcended states.

Capitalism, as Marx (1977) argued, pulls individuals out of constitutive communal bonds and declares them to be autonomous. But of course the autonomy is illusory; people find themselves subject to forces – like global markets – operating on a very large scale, and must confront these as individuals not only as members of communities. Reliance on large-scale categorical identities like nation is partially a response to this. This global order, moreover, is subject to recurrent global crises, and also produces localized crises each of which may be grasped by unattractive uses of nationalist discourse and violence in the name of national purification. The horrors of Rwanda and Burundi were shaped by various international pressures including wild swings in coffee and other commodity prices; those in the former Yugoslavia bear the imprint not only of the collapse of communism but of economic crisis.

Capitalism itself depended on and continually increased the capacity for large-scale and indirect social relations. Capitalism continually drove its agents out beyond local markets, established competitive pressures around the globe, and demanded coordination of ever-growing supplies of labour and raw materials – even before the generation of increasing consumer demand became an obsession. The nation became the domestic market; other nations became international competitors or clients.[9] The globalization wrought by capitalism also encouraged dramatic labour migrations. Political and economic factors intertwined, as migrants often fled nationalist strife, and their arrival in new settings contributed to xenophobic nationalist responses.

Capitalism is the greatest engine driving the expansion of global interconnections and large-scale organization generally. But unlike state formation, its impacts on nationalism have been mainly indirect. First, capitalism played a central role in creating systems so large and complex that local communities and other associations formed out of directly interpersonal relationships could not serve most people as adequate mediations. Second, capitalism directly undermined much of local community life, kinship and other social organization based on webs of direct, interpersonal relations (not making them disappear, but reducing their capacity to serve as basic building blocks of large-scale social organization). Third, capitalism encouraged individualism, organizing people mainly as owners of private property or sellers of labour power. The idea of nation is the most important of several categorical identities that step between the putatively autonomous (but on a global scale relatively weak) individual and the supremely complex and powerful forces of global social order (or disorder).

While capitalism played a central role in sundering certain forms of social connection, it also created new ones. Above all, it created the means for maintaining very indirect social relations on a large scale – paradigmatically through the market, but also through large administrative organizations like multinational corporations. Capitalism also facilitated and encouraged, though it does not by itself explain, the development of other forms of communication. Anderson (1991; see also Habermas 1989), for example, has called attention to the crucial role played by 'print capitalism' in the development of modern nationalism. Such early businesses and business-supporting ventures as newspapers, journals and even novels facilitated nationalism by helping to spread nationalist ideology and shared culture. In addition, their very form and the practice of reading them helped to reinforce a notion of social interconnection among the members of large-scale categories linked by only weak and not very dense social relationships (Calhoun 1991). Thus, as Anderson notes, readers of newspapers could imagine themselves as engaging in an activity which they shared with thousands or even millions of others. Small-scale businesses, adjuncts usually to the main dramas of capitalism, played an important role in promoting nationalist discourse by providing important bases for public life: coffee houses, publishing houses, etc. Communications infrastructures have facilitated space-transcending linkages which encouraged people to give up the narrow outlooks of their native villages for an understanding of themselves as (individually) members of the nation (Deutsch 1966, 1969; Schlesinger 1987).

Because more and more of the activity on which lives and livelihoods depended was taking place at a distance from each immediate locale, attempts to conceptualize the commonalities and connections among locales were increasingly important. Connections established only through markets and the commodity form were especially prone to reification and representation in categorical terms (Marx 1977; Postone 1993). Capital hired labour, thus, rather than businesses hiring workers. Class itself was such a categorical term. Above all, people situated themselves as members of various such categories in relation to 'the market', understood in reified terms as an all-encompassing environment rather than the product of human actions.

In markets, thus conceived, concrete social relations are seldom thematized. Buyers of shoes and sellers of socks do not confront each other as concrete persons engaged in direct exchange. Individuals enter the market, rather, as members of abstract categories of buyers and sellers – those with enough money to buy the best shoes, or those with so little bargaining position they must make socks at pitiful wages. They need have no particular social relations with the others in their category. Yet people are constantly addressed as members of such categories – by advertisers, for example, and indeed the producers of the media programmes supported by the advertisements. Commercials are targeted at potential consumers of expensive shoes; unionization campaigns at poorly paid sock-makers. As members of such categories people learn of the benefits and threats brought by changes in the market – minimum wage rates will rise; mortgage rates will fall; jobs like theirs will be lost to Japanese competition. As the last example suggests, national identities become vital categories in such representations. Indeed, although markets have never stopped at national borders and capital flows and other economic processes have long been international, everyday discourse continues to address people as members of national economies. It tells them to be grateful that 'the American economy' is showing signs of recovery, or worried because the American economy is being damaged by unfair international competition. It is only through our sense of ourselves as members of various such categories – mainly fairly large-scale ones – that we are able to situate ourselves in relation to the enormous, distant, impersonal forces (economic above all) that shape our lives. Nation is the most important of these – though religious identifications (sometimes overlapping with nationalism) are also powerful (see Jurgensmeyer 1993). The cultural politics of nationalism and religious fundamentalism are among the ways in which people respond indirectly to their incorporation into relatively large polities and a global economy in which power is real but mobilized from distant and sometimes obscure centres.

Equivalence and misrecognition

No nation-state ever existed entirely unto itself. As Tilly has shown, European states grew and intensified their administration in the context of a web of interstate rivalries (Tilly 1975, 1990). These were played out in economic as well as military and diplomatic arenas (though the politics of dynastic kinship and inheritance did not disappear until fairly late in the process). Gradually, from the early modern era through the nineteenth and early twentieth centuries, older political organizations like empires, quasi-autonomous principalities, and free cities gave way to a more standardized system. The world was divided into formally equivalent states, each of which was sovereign. Ideally, each of these states represented a single nation, hence the term 'nation-state'. By the second half of the twentieth century, it was clearly anomalous for any nation-state to remain under the explicit political tutelage of another, and where such relations existed they were commonly subjected to campaigns to undo them.[10]

Most nationalist movements have involved claims to states – either claims to create autonomous states where these do not exist or claims that the nation should govern a state currently in the hands of foreigners or other illegitimate rulers. Occasionally nationalists are prepared to settle for special recognition in the constitution of a multinational state. But the discourse of nationalism does not operate only in the direction of people to state; the reciprocal claim is also common. By the nineteenth century, Europeans thought not only that every nation deserved a state, thus, but that each state should represent one nation (Kohn 1968).

One feature of this new way of conceptualizing sovereignty is the treatment of all nation-states as formally equivalent, whatever their size or power. The discourse of nationalism demands that San Marino, two dozen square miles with 24,000 citizens, be seen as formally equivalent to China or the United States. It is a full member of the United Nations. The equivalence of states is emphasized especially in arenas like the UN, not only because the discourse of nationalism predominates, but because attention is paid to the whole system of states at once. Even in interstate relations where disparities of power and scale matter substantially, however, the rhetoric of equivalence is commonly observed. New York City may be more than twice as populous as Eritrea or Norway, say, but this does not grant it comparable diplomatic status; the United States, not subsidiary polities within it (like states or cities), relates to each other country as a peer.

At the same time that formal equivalence confers a certain dignity on a nation, this is unlikely to substitute for power and stature among nations; nationalism can turn to militarism, economic insularity, and concerns for slighted honour.[11] This can of course lead to war, and to a cycle of injuries, resentments and new conflicts (such as that in the Balkans). But the domestic, largely discursive, consequences of such international pursuits should not be ignored. International conflict generally, and military mobilization in particular, can help to confer (or enforce) unity on a disparate domestic population. As James Sheehan (1978: 279) writes of Germany after World War I, 'military defeat brought national humiliation and called into question the very existence of the nation which many in the middle strata saw as the ultimate political value and the last hope for political cohesion'. Remilitarization was a way to retrieve national unity – to save the nation domestically as well as internationally. The legitimacy and integrity of the contemporary state depended in part on the capacity to claim a strong national history. This fuelled both a reconsideration of the past and new action designed to fulfil the so-far empty promise of that past.

Similarly, in both Risorgimento and especially fascist Italy, a problematic past – lagging behind European neighbours, suffering losses in colonial wars – became the focus of enormous nationalist attention, as for example heroes of wars half-successful at best were redefined as national martyrs. In this process, as Mabel Berezin has noted, 'the fascist regime attempted to colonize the principle sources of Italian emotional attachment, family and religion, and submerge them in the community of the state' (Berezin 1997 and forthcoming). The Italian state encouraged pronatalist policies, for example, mobilizing ideas of romantic and familial love and images from the Virgin Mary to the spinster sacrificing herself for the nation to produce an emotionally compelling narrative of national cultural identity. It is not only in the Italian case that the production of a 'strong' nationalism has taken on a strikingly gendered character, promoting ideals of manhood and claiming certain forms of private life as essential to the nation. This has been true of other fascisms, and also of a variety of nationalisms (Mosse 1985; Parker *et al.* 1992). The removal of women from public life has been a striking feature, for example, of the replacement of communism by nationalism as a legitimating ideology in much of Eastern Europe and the former Soviet Union. A very gendered conception of the nation – and a strongly stereotyped vision of the role of women as members of the nation – figured in the French Revolution, and in such continuing imagery as 'Marianne', whose body – at once sexual and potentially maternal, yet not without a militant edge – embodied the French nation (Agulhon 1981; Hunt 1992).

The claim to a singular match between each state and its nation, reinforced by international jealousies, humiliations and fears, has often been the basis for both repression of difference within the nation (including non-orthodox gender roles) and attempts to exclude or subjugate all 'foreign' elements within the state (including the racially or ethnically distinct as well as actual immigrants; see Gilroy 1991). The language of national humiliation (or international abuse more generally) provides a discourse in which people can respond to felt problems, like impoverishment, without recognizing the extent to which their interests conflict with others of their countrymen. This misrecognition is not simply manipulated from above but built into the discourse of nationalism (on misrecognition, see Bourdieu 1990).

The existence of a world-system of states, in sum, constitutes a continuing pressure for the use of nationalist discourse in the justification of claims to sovereignty. Though some analysts predict the dissolution of such states in a postmodern welter of local identities and global corporations, the states do not yet seem to have given up the ghost. It is widely argued that the ability of states to maintain sharp boundaries and to promote internal cultural homogeneity is in decline. It is not clear how such a trend would affect nationalism. On the one hand, it would undermine the extent to which states were likely to be powerful agents of nationalism, and reduce the attractions of gaining state power. On the other hand, it would reduce the capacity of states to resist subsidiary nationalisms and increase the occasions for potentially nationalist groups to form. Not least of all, even if weakened, states are likely to remain the only institutional framework within which to pursue large-scale projects of democracy and self-determination. But at the same time, this world-system of states is recalcitrant to new claims for statehood, whether based on integration/amalgamation or on disintegration/secession. In the nineteenth-century 'Springtime of Nations', it could be assumed that the world-system of states could readily provide for every nation's freedom (Kohn 1968; Sheehan 1978; Szporluk 1988). That vision did not last long, though its rhetoric of self-determination still endures, partly because it was founded on the assumption that some clear primordial or historical basis could be found which would settle decisively the question of which were the true nations. As Gellner has remarked, however, 'on any reasonable calculation, the former number (of potential nations) is probably much, much larger than that of possible viable states' (1983: 2).[12] Not all potential nations pursued goals of nation building or state autonomy.

The world-system of nations is therefore both an incentive to nationalism and a constraint on it. It is an incentive because there is no other basis for participation in world affairs. And it is a constraint because its tacit assumption is always that the full complement of states is already represented. It therefore takes quite remarkable events to achieve international recognition for a new state. In Africa both political leaders and intellectuals routinely and rightly complain of the arbitrariness – or even insidiousness – of the boundaries drawn by European colonial powers. Ethnic groups were often split, traditional enemies thrown together, port access eliminated and trade routes ignored by Europeans dividing the continent amongst themselves, and sometimes trying to divide the natives in order to rule them better (Amin 1975; Nzongola-Ntalaja 1987). Yet post-colonial African governments and the Organization of African States have been extremely loath to recognize any secessionist regime, partly at least because they were all too aware of such possibilities at home (Lewis 1983; Mazrui and Tidy 1984; Davidson 1992). Not only the OAU but the United Nations refused to question Ethopia's annexation of Eritrea, dubious as it was, and out of self-interest as well as because of Ethiopian diplomacy (Iyob 1995; Selassie 1980, 1989). It is remarkable that Eritrea's 1992 independence marked the first success for a nationalist movement seeking to undo one of the partially arbitrary combinations of peoples and territories wrought in Africa by colonialism and international agreements, and maintained by modern African states.

Eritrea's pursuit of national autonomy through thirty years of war demonstrates the continuing importance of nationalism as a way of framing collective identity and political aspirations. The success of the Eritrean struggle, not only on the field of battle but in gaining international recognition, reminds us that the rhetoric of nationalism is still effective. The fact that the Eritrean struggle forged national identity where there was little history of ethnic unity points out the open-ended potential of nationalism. Nationalism is an option not only for advancing old solidarities but for creating new ones.

Conclusion

Nationalism is too diverse to allow a single general theory to explain it all. Much of the content and specific orientation of various nationalisms is determined by historically distinct cultural traditions, the creative actions of leaders, and contingent situations within the international order. What can be addressed in more general, theoretical terms are the factors that lead to the continual production and reproduction of nationalism as a central discursive formation in the modern world. These do not explain all the implications or characteristics of nationalist discourse, but they offer a first step in the attempt to understand why it exists and retains its importance.

Nationalism draws on cultural traditions and ethnicity, but neither its form nor its historically specific prevalence in the modern era is explained by these factors. Rather, it is necessary to look first and foremost at the ways in which nationalism constitutes a discursive formation that both shapes and attempts to cope with the rise of the modern state. One of the first aspects of this is the effort to secure widespread participation in state governance. Nationalism plays a crucial, though often unexamined, role in the modern discourse of political legitimacy. Legitimacy turns, in much of that discourse, on the extent to which specific institutions of rule represent or serve the interests of 'the people'; nationalism is the rhetoric or discourse in which attempts are made to establish who the relevant people are. Their categorical identity is constructed through the discourse of nationalism. Challenges to putatively illegitimate governments can then be brought forward in the name of the nation.

Processes of state formation play an important part in furthering the integration of nations and therefore the salience of national identities. Along with the development of better transport and communications infrastructures and the extension of market relations and expansion of production organizations, development of state administrative capacities greatly increases the interconnections among different regions of a country. As they do so, they undermine various quasi-autonomous local organizations and sometimes repress contending candidate nations. In the course of unifying a country, they establish greater levels of internal cultural commonality, including linguistic uniformity. Cultural similarities are seized upon in the constitution of categorical identities. The discourse of nationalism provides expression to this process. But as a discursive formation, nationalism shapes the form of representation, not its precise contents or level of inclusion. Thus nationalist rhetoric offers direct expression to the process of unification through representations of the encompassing nation claimed at the scale of the state or even beyond it. At the same time, nationalist rhetoric is also used to represent the opposing claims to autonomy on the part of subject peoples and those who refuse integration into growing nation-states.

In both state formation and independence movements, the discourse of nationalism prompts the attempt to secure a satisfactory fit between nation and state. This is made especially important by the political ideologies emphasizing citizenship, for the participation of citizens demands a kind of lateral connection to each other and a kind of exclusive loyalty to the state not required by empires and other older forms of polity. The claim to national 'self-determination', a staple of independence movements, is very closely tied to this discourse in which political legitimacy rises from the people, even though self-determination is sometimes claimed on behalf of a nation by elites with no intention of instituting democracy or any form of popular participation in government.

The issues of autonomy, self-determination and proper fit between nation and state necessarily are addressed only in the context of a world of other states. The organization of this world reflects, in part, the process of capitalist expansion with its partial separation between the units of economic and political organization. It reflects also the division of virtually the entire population and territory of the world into states (and their dominions), so that people can identify their place in the world, have some voice, and claim autonomy mainly through their membership in a nation and citizenship in a state. In Western Europe, the nationalist project centered on making state and nation coincide – by amalgamating and consolidating territory, and also by transforming populations from diverse provincials into more 'integrated' nationals. But the same European states often created colonial empires, each extending its state beyond its nation. This created a basic tension that helped to fuel new nationalist movements. While it is important to emphasize the domestic roots of the discourse of nationalism, nothing calls forth more compelling nationalist discourse and commitments than international conflicts, wars. While non-state economic actors (like multinational corporations) may expand their roles, states remain the main mechanism for attempting to regulate their activity and the only large-scale arenas in which to claim rights of participation. Interstate migrations also reinforce nationalism, both by provoking reactionary responses in some host countries and by contributing to the national consciousness of those who experience the crossing of borders. But above all, modern warfare has become inextricably tied to the idea of nation.

Finally, the modern discourse of national identity is closely linked to the idea of the individual. Nations are constructed as 'super-individuals' on the one hand and categories of equivalent individuals on the other. An immediate, direct relationship is posited between individuals and their nations; national identity assumes a special priority over other collective identities in the construction of personal identity. Membership in a nation is not derived from membership in any other collectivity – family, community, etc.; it may be reinforced by kinship or other network bonds, but it is of a different form and order. Invoking or giving voice to large-scale categorical identities enables the discourse of nationalism to situate people in the world order (or disorder). Membership in a nation is a mediation between the discrete individual and the impersonal forces that affect his or her life while remaining beyond the control of direct, interpersonal relationships. The power with which such categorical identities shape us reflects importantly the power we know that states and large-scale economic activity have over us.

The discourse of nationalism can be used in democratic attempts to manage those large-scale forces. As categorical identities, indeed, nations help answer the question of who is entitled to participate in a modern state, an embarrassing question for democratic theory since it involves the admission of exclusivity. National identity is also a source of solidarity to bind people together despite their differences, though it can easily slip into use as a 'trump card' against those differences. Though nationalism and democracy have been closely related in the modern era, there is nothing inherently democratic about nationalism. Proponents of malign – and indeed sometimes illusory – solutions to popular grievances often employ the discourse of nationalism. Not just advocates of ethnic cleansing or bellicosity towards neighbours, but those who use talk of national interest to deflect attention from self-interested domestic policies and those who support unlikely separatisms as bases for improbable economic development all rely on the emotional power which national identity carries. So do more admirable advocates of national solidarity, care for all the nation's members, and self-sacrifice in the common interest.

Nationalism moves people emotionally, not least because it provides a sense of location in a large and complex world and an enormous reach of history. It is crucial to grasp that nationalism is a positive source of meaning – and even sometimes inspiration – and of mutual commitment among very large groups of people. If it were merely illusion and manipulation it could not have the power that it does. But this discursive formation commonly leads even those with the noblest of goals to address their nations as perduring, nearly fixed identities moving through history rather than constructed within it. Such a view of the nation is apt to deny the exercise of power involved both in its construction and in its continued internal organization. Such a view is also apt to resist the heterodox claims of various individuals and groups within the nation – those who would remake it or ask of it space to live differently from the ways authorized in dominant nationalist ideologies.

Solutions to the problems suggested in the preceding paragraph will require much future work. Such future work will depend, however, on understanding why the idea of nation and claims to national identity are so basic to modern politics and culture, and on recognizing the difference between the highly general nationalist discourse that shapes the modern era and the numerous and heterogeneous specific movements, policies, ideologies and conflicts that are constituted through use of that discourse.

Notes

Introduction

1 No definition of nation (or of its correlative terms such as nationalism and nationality) has ever gained general acceptance (Smith 1973, 1983; Alter 1989; Motyl 1992; Connor 1994; Hall 1995).

Chapter 1

1 '*Natio* in ordinary speech originally meant a group of men belonging together by similarity of birth, larger than a family, but smaller than a clan or a people.... The term applied particularly to a community of foreigners' (Kedourie 1994: 5).

2 On the history of map-making generally, see Thrower (1996). A stimulating, brief discussion of the relationship between map-making and nationalism may be found in Anderson (1991: Chapter 10).

3 The modern income tax, for example, dates from the efforts of the British Prime Minister, William Pitt the Younger, to raise the money needed to build and modernize the navy (as well as to strengthen the army) in order to resist Napoleon. The income tax required a high level of administrative capacity and information about the nation as a whole; it also linked each paying citizen directly to the state. This is only one of a number of ways in which the Napoleonic Wars helped to consolidate the modern nation-state ideology and the social organization that underpinned it. More generally, Britain's superior fiscal capacity was a key source of its international strength – including military power (Brewer 1989).

4 Du Bois (1989) contested this notion early on with his concept of 'double consciousness', though he focused especially on some of the difficulties such 'doubleness' brought to black Americans. For a more general

extension of this line of thought, showing also ways in which nationalist thought has shaped thinking about racial identity, see Gilroy (1993).

5 Talk of being 'at home' was one of the ways in which Martin Heidegger's philosophy resonated with the urges that were mobilized by Nazism. An emphasis on 'public space' was one of the crucial ways in which Heidegger's former student Hannah Arendt distinguished her philosophy from her teacher's. Attentive to the Heideggerian side of nationalism, Guibernau explains it by asserting that 'modern societies produce some kind of ontological insecurity as a consequence of the uncertainty and fragmentation that lie at their core' (1996: 134). That people need identity, however, does not tell us why they fixate on any particular scale or definition of identity. People may indeed seek sources of ontological security when faced with social contradictions and an unpredictable world, but people have faced insecurities throughout history, and found solace in families, communities, and religions as well as nations – and indeed have responded by entering public space as well as by seeking to feel at home.

6 See Hall (1995) among several discussions of the difficulty of theorizing all of the manifestations of nationalism – as distinct from producing a taxonomy of nationalisms and theories (plural) of different dimensions of nationalism. The same is true of marxism, as a nonacademic discipline and/or interdiscipinary field. As Nairn (1977) has argued, marxism has failed to produce a serious theory of nationalism despite (or perhaps because of) the fact that the international working-class movement met its most basic failures in competition with the early-twentieth-century appeal of nationalism (see also Debray 1977; Connor 1984). Anderson (1991: 3) has suggested that 'it would be more exact to say that nationalism has proved an uncomfortable *anomaly* for Marxist theory and, precisely for that reason, has been largely elided rather than confronted'.

7 Indeed, one of the biggest debates in socialist circles concerned whether revolutionary plans needed to be internationally coordinated or could proceed by means of the spontaneous mass risings predicted by Rosa Luxemburg and other theorists. After the Russian Revolution, the Bolsheviks used their domination of the international socialist movement to oppose 'spontaneous action' and mass risings. Though in principle committed to communist internationalism, the USSR began increasingly (especially under Stalin and after Trotsky's fall) to pursue a path of 'socialism in one country' which was heavily shaped by Russian (and/or Soviet) nationalism and which led Moscow to minimize aid to many revolutionaries elsewhere. See Claudin (1977).

8 Of course nationalist movements have occurred throughout the nineteenth and twentieth centuries; they have not been limited to those

periods when geopolitical upheavals and collapse of empires brought waves of such movements. The Palestinian struggle for an autonomous nation-state, for example, has continued with ebbs and flows since the creation of the modern Jewish state of Israel. Similarly, the Afghan nationalist struggle, influenced by Islamic revival, preceded the 1989 crisis of communism and indeed helped to weaken the Soviet State (just as the Eritrean nationalist movement which gathered force in opposition to feudal–imperial Ethiopia continued in conflict when Ethiopia became a Soviet client state and helped to doom the communist–nationalist government of the 'dergue' led by Mengistu Haile Mariam).

9 The argument that grievances are not enough to produce social movements is one of the main points of 'resource mobilization theory', which emphasizes that people always have grievances, and variation in their extent explains movements less than variations in capacities of organizers to produce concerted action, to communicate with followers, to secure material resources, etc. See McCarthy and Zald (1976); Oberschall (1973); Tilly (1978). The resource mobilization argument, however, sheds little light on the question of why movements are organized with an emphasis on certain specific constellations of identities, grievances, values, and claims. In other words, it leaves cultural factors unaddressed. It helps us understand why some nationalist movements may flourish and others fail, and why they come in waves at certain times, but not why they are *nationalist*.

10 Michael Hechter's (1975) argument about the ways in which internal colonialism and economic underdevelopment coincide to produce nationalism on Britain's 'Celtic fringe' is thus powerful with regard to the kind of factors resource mobilization theory considers, and weaker at explaining why nationalism became the preferred rhetorical frame for grasping grievances and formulating goals and complaints. The latter kinds of issues require understanding in terms of the historical construction and dissemination of the discourse of nationalism – and its embodiment both in the English-dominated British state and in successful examples elsewhere.

11 Social movements tend not to occur in isolation. Studies that focus on a single movement at a time – whether class, religious, nationalist, gender-based, or other – miss the embeddedness of each movement within a field of movements; see Calhoun (1993a). Tactics are shared by example and by the involvement of individuals in more than one movement – simultaneously or over time. The very existence of many movements, if they meet with even modest success, encourages the idea that collective action can in fact change the world and will not necessarily meet with repression. This 'cognitive liberation' is important to social movements in general (see McAdam 1982, 1986).

12 Complaining about this tendency to treat nationalism – and ethnicity more generally – as a special case or minor factor in world history, Daniel Patrick Moynihan (1993: 10–11) writes: 'there are today just eight states on earth which both existed in 1914 and have not had their form of government changed by violence since then. These are the United Kingdon, four present or former members of the Common-wealth, the United States, Sweden, and Switzerland. Of the remaining 170 or so contemporary states, some are too recently created to have known much recent turmoil, but for the greater number that have done, by far the most frequent factor involved has been ethnic conflict. Yet it is possible to have studied international relations through the whole of the twentieth century and hardly to have noticed this'.

13 Erica Benner (1995) has developed a strong account of Marx's and Engels' insights, which suggests what their analysis of nationalism might look like if they had given it the proper weight of sustained attention. See also the broader review of marxist approaches in Nimni (1991).

Chapter 2

1 The term 'primordial' enters this discussion from the work of Edward Shils (especially 1957).

2 See also Davidson (1992). As Ekeh (1990) has noted, there has been a move to abandon the use of 'tribe' in social anthropology and African studies, and to replace it with 'ethnic group'. Where the notion of tribe pointed to the centrality of kin relations (all the more central, Ekeh suggests, because of weak African states from whose point of view 'tribal-ism' is criticized), the notion of ethnic group implies that detailed, serious analysis of kinship is more or less irrelevant. This has the effect of imposing a categorical notion – a collection of individuals marked by common ethnicity – in place of a relational one.

3 Trevor-Roper (1983) points out how even so basic a symbol of national identity as the Highland Scot's kilt is largely a matter of reconstruction and invention in the context of Scots resistance to English domination; it only became widespread in the early eighteenth century.

4 Anderson (1991: 6) finds the same fault with Gellner: 'Gellner is so anxious to show that nationalism masquerades under false pretences that he assimilates "invention" to "fabrication" and "falsity", rather than to "imagining" and 'creation".'

5 This is a sociological proposition as old as W.I. Thomas's principle that what we believe to be true is true for us (see elaboration in Merton 1968). It is given more substantial theoretical underpinnings in Pierre Bourdieu's (1976, 1990) analyses of the reproduction of culture as both cognitive content and prediscursive, embodied orientations to the

world. As Edward Shils (1981) has suggested, we should see tradition not just as the relatively fixed contents of culture, but as the active process of 'passing on'. See also Calhoun (1983).

6 In other words, they are literally prejudices in Hans-Georg Gadamer's (1975, 1977) sense. Prejudice means not just prior to judgment, but constituting the condition of judgment. Existence within a historical tradition opens the possibility of knowing the world, it is not just a source of narrowing or historical error; see Warnke (1987). Yet, equally, traditions are effective only when they are living and therefore changing; they derive their force from their efficacy in opening an understanding of the world that works in practical action, not from offering an empirically demonstrable claim to a specific original truth.

7 In Bourdieu's (1976, 1990) language, we can distinguish heterodoxy, or recognition of multiple beliefs as legitimate, not only from orthodoxy but from a 'doxic' attitude in which adherence is unquestioningly presupposed. The reproduction of cultural tradition is supported by social practices that discourage or limit experimentation with alternatives, and inhibit searches for other ways of seeing things. Ethnicity embeds us in a web of such practices and in a social group which constantly reproduces them and may view any challenge to them as disloyalty.

8 Arguments over antiquity matter rather more in appeals to external audiences, including the International Court of Justice and similar bodies. See Gebre-Ab (1993); Iyob (1995) and Selassie (1989) on Eritrea.

9 This does not mean that nationalism erases the importance of all other identities (any more than that trump cards are played in every trick of a bridge game). It means that nationalist discourse exerts a powerful force against ideals such as that which John Schwarzmantel (1991: 5) ascribes to socialism: 'the socialist idea of the nation is or ought to be a "pluralistic" one, seeing national identity as one focus of loyalty among others, and rejecting the idea of the nation put forward by "integral" nationalism, in which the nation is seen as the supreme and overriding focus of loyalty, to which all other affiliations must be totally subordinate'. Nationalist discourse generally accepts that other affiliations may occupy the primary attention of good members of a nation much of the time, but grants these other affiliations no right to challenge the nation in matters of basic importance.

10 Kin, in a general sense, are those to whom one is related by sharing either descent from a common ancestor or connection through marriage. Kinship, thus, can be used inclusively to refer to the whole set of relationships and identities formed by affinal and consanguinal ties – 'in-laws' and 'blood'. Anthropologists frequently distinguish the two,

however, because descent often has a very specific role in the formation of group identities distinct from the broader range of kin relations.

11 This contrast is brought out especially clearly in Evans-Pritchard's (1940) classic ethnography of the Nuer. See also the more general systematization in Nadel (1957). Harrison White has been largely responsible for bringing this conceptualization into contemporary sociological usage. Unfortunately this is partly oral tradition from his teaching, for he never published his own influential early paper on the subject (but see White 1992). See also Calhoun (1991).

12 When nationalist rhetoric is used to describe a group within a country, it means that the user is claiming that the smaller group is the real nation, and the larger country is multinational or not a nation. Thus a Scot may recognize that Scotland is, at the moment, part of a larger country called Britain, but claim that 'Briton' is not a legitimate nationality (or is another name for English). He or she would consider Scotland – and presumably Wales and England – to be nations, but Great Britain to be a multinational state.

13 Among the Romans, the use of *natio*, the root of 'nation', was equivalent to ethnicity in this sense; it meant simply people of common ancestry and thereby common character.

14 Indeed, in larger, multi-ethnic societies ethnic groups have tended to have less and less thorough organization in terms of kinship and descent. The category of common ethnicity has remained important, as has family at the lower levels of lineage and intermarriage, but the whole system of kinship has become less complete than, say, for the traditional Tallensi.

15 The Ethiopian (Amharic) term, 'falasha', actually means strangers, and thus carries a derogatory connotation. It has nonetheless become widely used, and standard among Ethiopians. The word 'falasha' is used by Christian Ethiopians to designate the Jews as outsiders, even though Falasha are descendants of ancient Ethiopians. Indeed, the ancient kingdom of Axum, an important predecessor to what is today Ethiopia, was predominantly Jewish in the time of the Queen of Sheba (Makeda) – 1500 or 1600 BC. In the fifth century after Christ its rulers converted to Christianity – and in many cases became quite fanatical about it. They fought with Jews from the Arabian peninsula (part of which Axum ruled) and with local Jews who resisted the abandonment of Judaism for Christianity. From the fifth century AD, apparently, and with renewed force in the next century, the Jews – though of basically the same racial stock and ethnic origins as other locals – began to be seen (and stigmatized) as outsiders (see Marcus 1994).

16 This problem is apparent in Weber's (1976) construction of the idea of traditional authority. China was also more dynamic than common usage

of 'traditional' allows, but Confucian understandings of Chinese imperial authority did emphasize an account of patriarchy which knitted together an entire society through kinship and descent. Particularly in periods when the imperial bureaucracy and *junxian* market system were ascendant over *fengjian* militarism and feudal lords this meant that overall societal integration was conceived as fully on the kinship and descent model as anywhere (Schrecker 1991).

17 This is part of the point of the commodification of labour and the reduction of skill differentiations that, Marx argued, made all workers competitors with each other in capitalist production relations and allowed capitalists to drive down the price of labour. Likewise, though, capitalists were ultimately interchangeable as the 'job' of management was separated from the property-relation of ownership, and as the demands of the market place forced capitalists to compete with each other, innovate, hold their costs down, and generally adhere to the demands of a larger, standardizing capitalist system or face bankruptcy (and disappearance as capitalists).

18 Schwarzmantel (1991: 37–40) somewhat misleadingly portrays Fichte's idea of the nation as simply a domination and total absorption of the individual, rather than seeing the sense in which Fichte sees self-recognition and self-realization as having non-contradictory individual and national moments.

19 This is the sort of transformation Marx had in mind when he discussed the movement from 'class in itself' to 'class for itself', though the dialectic seems to have been more effective in the case of nations.

20 Jürgen Habermas (1992, 1994, 1996), for example, presents the idea of 'constitutional patriotism' as an alternative to ethnically defined nationalism. Locke (1950) prefigured this opposition by distinguishing the public realm from family, precisely on the grounds that the former could be a matter of reasoned choice while the latter must be a matter of pre-rational commitment.

21 Richard Madsen (1995: x) tells the story of a mainland Chinese general who argued that it was obvious that Taiwan had no plausible claim to independence because 'the people on Taiwan speak Chinese, their culture is Chinese, their ancestors came from mainland China. Therefore they are Chinese, and Taiwan should be a part of China'. Madsen's rejoinder was: 'If our forefathers truly agreed with such an argument, we would still be part of England'.

Chapter 3

1 It fell from use under anti-nationalist influences during the later 1960s

and 1970s, and in the 1990s is making a comeback under conservative sponsorship in more chauvinistic times.

2 More common than the attempt to explain nationalism by ethnicity is the functionalist argument that it is mainly a carry-over from an earlier, more genuinely ethnically structured 'gemeinschaft', maintained as a defence against the disruption of traditional communities and systems of meaning (Geertz 1963; Gellner 1964; Hayes's 1966 treatment of nationalism on the model of religion is similar). Such treatments owe a great deal to Durkheim's (1984) account of the transition from mechanical to organic solidarity, as this passage from Haas (1964: 465) makes clear:

> The nation is a synthetic *Gemeinschaft*. In the mass setting of modern times, it furnishes the vicarious satisfaction of needs that have previously been met by the warmth of small, traditional, face-to-face social relations. As social life has been transformed by industrialization and social mobilization into something resembling a *Gesellschaft* based on interest calculations, the nation and nationalism continue to provide the integrative cement that gives the appearance of community.

Mauss's (1985) unfinished writings on nationalism, shaped significantly by the same orientation, show a greater recognition of the force of the category of nation as a shaping influence in modern culture.

3 Though not a political nationalist, Herder (1966) founded this approach to language; Fichte fused it with political nationalism. It is perhaps no accident that both historical approaches to language and textual hermeneutics have been particularly German academic contributions while 'structural' accounts of language and the severing of texts from their origins have been distinctively popular in France. The extent to which Saussure's structuralism prospered in French thought as against German historicism is an often overlooked aspect of theoretical history. This is congruent with the fact that the French obsession with linguistic purity, so commonly noted today, is of relatively recent origin, largely as a late-nineteenth-century response to colonialism, recalcitrant language groups in France, and the internationalization of culture. The official enforcer of linguistic purity, the Academie Française, moreover, works not on etymological or historical principles but on criteria of internal fit, or elegance, a kind of implicit structuralism. (It also admits members of foreign origin on the basis of the quality of their French, something hard to imagine in Germany given the ethnic–historical construction of German linguistic consciousness.)

4 See also Meinecke (1970: 92). This two-stage model is similar to Connor's (1994: 103) distinction of ethnic groups as 'potential nations'

from real nations: 'While an ethnic group *may*, therefore, be other-defined, the nation *must* be self-defined'.

5 Independence – not just formal, but realized in autonomy of action and protection from pernicious external influences – is the crucial good that can be elevated to transcendent status to justify the miseries and personal losses of war. No sum of individual interests allows the calculation that sacrifice was worthwhile (no mother would set a personal price as adequate compensation for lost sons or daughters). Economic gains, for example, are both less exalted and, in the Eritrean case, rather harder so far to see.

6 There was even a special name for such Krajina or 'Frontier' Serbs.

7 While some nationalists are deeply and enduringly committed to placing nationalism in the forefront of their consciousness, most people are moved more intermittently and inconsistently by nationalist sentiments which vie with other feelings and interests in their personal agendas. As one analyst of the Serb situation could assert by 1996, 'Nationalism is no longer fashionable. Its place has been taken by Yugo-nostalgia' (Dobbs 1996).

8 Eventually, ironically, Milosevic would be subject to attack from more extreme and less pragmatic nationalists who asserted that he sold out Bosnian Serbs by accepting the US-brokered Dayton accord. Protests beginning in late 1996 mingled claims to democracy with strident nationalism. The independent radio station B92 symbolized the attractive side of this rebellion to Westerners – first banned as a base of dissidents then coming back stronger than ever and complete with its own Web site. At the same time, perhaps the most visible domestic leader of the protests was the rock singer Bora Djordjevic, who accused the President of 'betrayal of the Serbs in Croatia and Bosnia'. 'Being a Serb is everything to me now', Djordjevic told one Western reporter, then went on to reveal the centrality of religion to Serb nationalism: 'I have become extremely religious. I'd be lost without religion. I have to believe there is something else, something better.' Yet Djordjevic too was a recent convert to the nationalist cause, a former anti-communist rebel who previously sang that 'only fools die for ideals'. Sasa Mirkovic, the manager of radio B92, saw nationalist ideology saving Djordjevic's popularity (much as it saved Milosevic's political power). 'When Yugoslavia fell apart the popularity of rock bands like [Djordjevic's] Fish Soup began to decline, and the steeper the decline the more Djordjevic became a Serbian nationalist' (Hedges 1997: 4).

Chapter 4

1 The most sustained recent accounts of the relationship of nationalism

to state formation are in Mann (1986, 1993) and Breuilly (1993). See also the influential earlier work of Deutsch (1966, 1969) and Kohn (1968). On state formation more generally, see Poggi (1973); Anderson (1974); Tilly (1975); Giddens (1984) and Tilly (1990).

2 Gellner's (1983) arguments that industrialization wrought nationalism are narrower, but in this vein. Polanyi (1944) is a classic account stressing markets generally more than just industry. See also Balibar and Wallerstein (1991).

3 Indeed, the usage was even more distant from contemporary national identities (Kedourie 1994: 5–7). The medieval University of Paris had four 'nations': France (including all speakers of romance languages), Picardie (basically, the Dutch and Flemish), Normandie (meaning mainly Scandinavians), and Germanie (which included speakers of English as well as German).

4 Martin Luther's famous 'Open Letter to the Christian Nobility of the German Nation' uses the term primarily in its medieval sense, describing the elites who might attend Church councils, but such documents in the Lutheran Reformation anticipated more modern usage of the word 'nation'. This is so principally because they appealed to an entire linguistically and culturally defined people and were widely distributable because of the growth of vernacular literacy (enhanced in considerable measure by the Lutheran Bible that Johannes Gutenburg printed and encouraged by the circulation of documents like Luther's 'Open Letter'). In his key nationalist 'Addresses' of 1807–8, Fichte (1968) evokes Luther, but the usage is clearly modern.

5 Descending theories were epitomized by divine right legitimations of sovereignty. Ascending theories, on the other hand, foreshadowed the birth of the more modern idea of nation or people with their notion that sovereignty was a grant of the people to the ruler. Claiming that this was crucial to ancient Germany, and invoking Althusius, Gierke (1934) used this as a rationale for arguments against absolutist rule and the domination of state over society. In general, the emerging ideas of nation and public drew heavily on both Roman Republican legal ideas and the discourse of natural law (Ullman 1977).

6 For a compelling account of the role of republican ideas in a crucial early moment of modern political transformation, see Pocock (1975). See also Hunt (1984) and Blum (1986) on the French construction of the republican *patrie*. Even modern monarchical states have been shaped by republican ideas. Of course, republicanism is not altogether new, as the example of Rome reminds us; Rome reminds us also that transitions from republic to empire are also possible. These have occurred in the modern era as, for example, when the Union of Soviet Socialist Republics without announcement constituted itself in significant ways as

an empire, both internally (with relation to the non-Russian republics) and externally (with relation to Warsaw pact dependencies).

7 As Chatterjee (1994), has argued, this became a crucial issue in the way in which Europeans conceptualized the peoples they subjected to colonial rule. The British in India, for example, found it very important to claim that indigenous India did not constitute a single society but rather a melange of heterogeneous and conflict-prone communities. This view legitimated the Raj, but it also provided one of the incentives for Indian elites interested in opposing British hegemony to develop nationalist claims about the unity of India (which, in turn, were among the factors that exacerbated Hindu–Muslim tensions).

8 Hegel looms too large in the most prominent recent general account of the political theory of civil society (Cohen and Arato 1992). This obscures the importance of Scottish, English and French analyses, and of the extent to which the discourse had from the beginning an emphasis on capacity for non-state social organization. This discourse was, of course, a crucial forerunner to the constitution of sociology. See Calhoun (1993b).

9 It should be clear that neither France nor England (let alone Britain) was religiously homogeneous. The religious unity of the nation was in part an ideological imposition – as are all claims to singular, integral national identity. But it was a powerful one. French Protestants were slaughtered and driven into exile in the name of national unity, creating among other things the Huguenot communities of North America. Anti-popery mobs remained a commonplace of English popular politics (especially in times of war with France) until well into the nineteenth century. The anti-Catholicism of the American Ku Klux Klan was not only a response to Southern European immigrants but an inheritance of this defining feature of Anglo-Saxon identity.

10 And in this sense, we see more of the modern notion of the people in relation to the state in the early histories of both Judaism and Islam than in either the Greece or Rome of classical antiquity, however beloved of early modern political theorists these were.

11 Paradoxically, Hobbes's account anticipated the tradition of civic nationalism associated most commonly with the French Revolution. Though Hobbes's theory supported monarchy rather than revolution, it suggested that any individual conforming to the institutions of political rule could be a member of the body politic. It was assimilationist rather than ethnicist.

12 Kohn (1968) remains perhaps the best treatment of this dimension of the origins of English nationalism. See also Greenfeld (1992), though note that she gives remarkably little attention to the extent to which the aristocratic proponents of nation against king were opponents of the

more democratic assertions of the rights of Englishmen by Levellers, Diggers and others.

13 This said, we should not exaggerate the extent of 'assimilation' within European states. Bretons and Corsicans, for example, suggest the limits of cultural and political integration in France. See Noiriel (1996). Connor (1994: 183) rightly faults Karl Deutsch and other theorists who associate nationalism overwhelmingly with state building for neglecting the resistance to assimilation on the part of Flemings, Scots, Welsh and other national groups subordinated by still (if not explicitly) multi-cultural European states. Deutsch had treated all these groups as successfully assimilated, and presented not only France but Italy, Spain, and Switzerland as states with a single national consciousness. The resurgence of 'sub-state' ethnic nationalism encouraged by the formation of the European Community adds to the evidence that assimilation is not complete and cultural diversity always available to those who see material advantage or other attractions to the project of emphasizing it. See Schlesinger (1992); Delanty (1995) and Guibernau (1996).

14 *Encyclopédie* (Paris, 1751–65), Vol. 11, p. 36; my translation.

15 Michael Walzer (1983, 1992) constitutes an honourable exception to this tendency. Joining in the recognition of this limitation (though in his case not to democratic theory *per se* but to the theory of justice) John Rawls (1993) has taken up the question of what 'rights' might mean among nations, or what might legitimately constitute a 'law of peoples'.

16 Greenfeld's (1992) account of both seventeenth century England and the arguments for not seeing nationalism earlier is helpful; compare Marcu (1975), Armstrong (1982).

17 See Blum (1986). Even earlier, Montesquieu's ([1748] 1976) appeal to the 'spirit' of laws had presaged a modern discourse of national cultures and characters.

18 See, for example, the insightful discussions of the ways in which nationalist ideologues have tried to impose certain standards of proper sexual behaviour in Mosse (1985) and Parker *et al.* (1992).

19 See Walker Connor's (1994: Chapter 7) strictures against 'ahistoricalness'.

Chapter 5

1 In India, for example, the word 'nationalism' is used for all-India movements and ideologies, a heritage of anti-colonial struggle and especially the programme of the Congress Party. Otherwise similar (and in the broadest sense nationalist) programmes put forward by smaller groups – e.g. Sikhs, Hindus or Muslims – are termed 'communal'.

2 See Nairn's (1977) dismissal of such liberal theories, with their neglect of internal conflict and struggle. For a recent attempt to resuscitate and reconstruct the liberal theory, see Tamir (1993).

3 Great sociological theorists were not immune to this tendency. Max Weber was overcome with enthusiasm during an early stage of World War I, writing that 'no matter what the outcome, this war is really great and wonderful beyond all expectations' (Marianne Weber 1988: 528). Weber also expressed enthusiasm for 'the historical tasks of the German nation' and took it for granted that 'the vital interests of the nation stand, of course, above democracy and parliamentarianism' (Max Weber 1976: 1394, 1383). Of course Weber was not naively supportive of every military goal, and challenged the expansionist annexation plans of many in the faction seeking unity for 'Greater Germany'. On Weber and German nationalism see Mommsen (1984); Beetham (1985).

4 The existence of this 'civic' dimension to German nationalism is precisely what allows Jürgen Habermas to propose 'constitutional patriotism' as the best path of future German (and possibly European) development. Habermas in effect suggests expanding the extent to which German nationalism is organized in terms of loyalty to the political state and its constitution and reducing its ethnic dimension. See Habermas (1992, 1994, 1996).

5 In both France and Britain, nineteenth-century colonial experiences reshaped attitudes toward language. The first chairs of English were established at Indian universities, but the notion soon spread to Britain itself. The *Academie Française* became an agent of linguistic standardization (rather than simply a Pantheon of living literary deities) under the influence not only of the Enlightenment, but of state-making and educational reform.

6 Ironically, the very successful integration of the French nation-state may have predisposed France to its succession of republican revolutions – all of which not only claimed popular legitimacy but were made possible by the concentration of state power in a handful of spatially centralized institutions that could be seized by revolutionaries (Calhoun 1988).

7 Anderson (1991: 47) reminds us, however, that among the earliest clearly nationalist movements were those of Latin American creole elites who spoke the same language as the colonial power against which they rebelled.

8 Quoted in *Le Monde*, 1 October 1991.

9 Compare the misunderstanding in Barber (1995), where Islam is conceived as small-scale and relatively homogeneous, and Islamic fundamentalism as simply a reaction to globalization, aimed mainly at the

West, rather than part of a struggle over the character and future of Islam itself.

10 As Anderson (1991) suggests, sensibility to parallel histories reflected not only growing awareness of the broader world, but growing familiarity with written narratives, including both histories and novels. The latter were of importance in spreading the notion of simultaneous events embedded within different subnarratives – e.g. organized around different threads of a story or around different characters.

11 'Ren' means people or persons; *Zhongguoren* is more or less 'Chinese nation (or kingdom) people'. There are a number of other terms and combinations of terms that figured in the Chinese effort to come up with an adequate vocabulary of national identity. For example, the term *minzu*, derived from the traditional word for fellow clan members, was extended to become a term for nation. This could be the 'nation' of speakers of Chinese language, *Zhonghua minzu*, as well as the political nation.

12 It is also true that Chinese ideology typically exaggerates this unity. Not only is there deep linguistic diversity among Han Chinese, there are ethnic minorities that are far from tiny. Minorities make up less than 10 per cent of the Chinese population, but this still amounts to well over 80 million people. Some of the larger minorities have populations larger than most European nations. China's communists first courted national minorities with talk of their self-determination, then reversed themselves on achieving power, as the following text from October 1949 reveals:

> Today the question of each minority's 'self-determination' should not be stressed any further. In the past, during the period of civil war, for the sake of strengthening the minorities' opposition to the Guomindang's reactionary rule, we emphasized this slogan. This was correct at the time. But today the situation has fundamentally changed ... For the sake of completing our state's great purpose of unification, for the sake of opposing the conspiracy of imperialists and other running dogs to divide China's national unity, we should not stress this slogan in the domestic nationality question and should not allow its usage by imperialists and reactionary elements among various domestic nationalities ... The Han occupy the majority population of the country, moreover, the Han today are the major force in China's revolution. Under the leadership of the Chinese Communist Party, the victory of China's people's democratic revolution mainly relied on the industry of the Han people.
>
> (quoted in Gladney 1990: 70)

13 Fanon (1965) argued that it was precisely through such bloody struggles

that post-colonial nations *must* be made, because only this shared shedding of blood would forge the necessary unity.

Chapter 6

1 Though their realm was certainly of imperial scale, to the extent that they were interested in promoting a unity between nation and state, the 'emperors' of China are in a sense miscategorized by that Western term; they bear more resemblances to absolutist monarchs like Louis XIV than to the Holy Roman Emperor or his ancient Roman ancestors.

2 Mann (1993); more generally, Mann (1995, pp. 49–50) has suggested, 'We cannot predict which few nations successfully emerged on the basis merely of "ethnicity". The presence or absence of regional administration offers a much better predictor'.

3 Eritrea presents a complex but instructive case. Ethiopian and Islamic cultures had contended with each other for centuries on the land that is now Eritrea. The country's highlands had closer ties to Christian elites in Ethiopia, the lowlands were both mainly Islamic and linked by trade into a broader range of international influences. From the late nineteenth century, Italian colonial rule gave the country its territorial definition and increased internal cohesion. Though there was some resistance to Italians, Eritrean nationalism became a substantial movement only after World War II, when Ethiopia campaigned, successfully, to have the colony of defeated Italy given to it. Ethiopia claimed Eritrea partly on the basis of historical links (though these were mainly to the highlands) but sought control especially because of Eritrea's ports (located in the lowlands). At this point, Eritrean nationalists were mostly Muslims, and were influenced by international Arab nationalist discourse. Ethiopia's rulers were engaged in their own transition from more traditional empire to nationalism, however, which included forcing Amharic (the language of the governing elite ethnic group) onto the rest of the country, including Eritrea. When highland Eritrean Christians found their own language, Tigrinya, banned along with others, and suffered both discrimination and heavy-handed military rule, they joined the previously mainly Muslim nationalist movement in increasing numbers. The mixture of the two groups during thirty years of war for independence helped to forge a new, more fully shared sense of national identity. See Markakis (1987) and Iyob (1995).

4 It would produce contorted prose to write without using the word 'culture' as though it referred to singular and relatively bounded individual cultures, but I hope readers will realize that I do not mean to suggest this. On the problems involved with the notion of simple 'translation'

across cultures or modularity of discursive formations, see Calhoun (1995: Chapter 2).

5 The idea that Third World, non-Western peoples were incapable of self-rule through nation-states has been widespread – together with its corollary that these 'underdeveloped' countries needed some manner of tutelage for a time (Blaut 1987). This idea figured not just in the open ideologies of colonialists but in aspects of modernization theory, and even in some of the approach of Great Russians towards Asian peoples in the Soviet Union. Chatterjee (1986, 1994) discusses this dimension of colonial ideology and nationalist response in the context of Indian history. The claim of disunity seems immediately more plausible in the case of India (and various African colonies) than in China, for example. Nonetheless, even though Western imperialists in China confronted an indigenous imperial regime capable of organizing administration in far-flung provinces, the theme of indigenous disunity and incapacity for self-organization was not entirely absent. It was given force by various peasant rebellions in the nineteenth century, including that of the Taipings, and by the internal conflicts among elites during the declining years of the Qing dynasty (including especially those between Han Chinese and their Manchu rulers). In the years of the Republic and warlords after 1911, the reality of internal division and consequent weakness impressed and shaped Chinese nationalism as well as imperialist opinion. Among other things, this intersection of imperialist ideology and domestic concern may have joined with ancient fears of chaos and faith in unity to reinforce nationalist desires for a strongly unified rather than a federal China. See discussion in Duara (1988, 1992).

6 Chatterjee writes sometimes as though the development of the concept of 'nation' in Western thought had remained more completely within the realm of specifically political discourse than it did. Thus he argues that the 'suppression in modern European social theory of an independent narrative of community . . . makes possible both the posing of the distinction between state and civil society and the erasure of that distinction' (1994: 283). This overgeneralizes, however, since the narrative of community has been a widespread and basic constituent of European social theory. Until the recent development of 'communitarianism', however, this was one of the main distinctions of *social* theory from political theory, especially in the English-language literatures. Political theory often suppressed consideration of communities other than the nation (a community of the whole), in favour of accounts relating individuals to states. Political theory lacked a strong account of social integration other than that accomplished by states; this paved the way for the recent 'rediscovery' of civil society as a theme in liberal political theory (see, e.g., Cohen and Arato 1992).

7 Aimée Césaire (1955) addressed similar issues within the context of the

same international movement of 'negritude', though with considerably less critical perspective on gender and patriarchy.

8 As Chatterjee (1994) shows, the term *jati* could be mobilized in such a way that it emphasized Indian or Hindu as the basic 'kind' into which a person fitted, rather than only the more specific and hierarchically arranged categories we associate with the term caste. Caste itself appeared largely as a categorical identity, part of a classificatory scheme that located individuals discretely. India was thus not quite so radically 'other' to the Western versions of categorical identities and individuals as is sometimes suggested. At the same time, many Western commentators distort actual practices when they approach caste as though it were a single scheme of classification holistically integrated at an all-India level (they bring in a nationalist consciousness without realizing it). Caste should also refer to a welter of local practices and groupings, many with greater relational, including kinship foundations and less clear-cut integration into any supra-local, national scheme of classification than the stereotype suggests. (I am indebted to Lee Schlesinger for discussions on this point and the opportunity to read unpublished writings.)

9 While capitalism occasioned both this kind of internal integration and this boundary maintenance, it did not in itself dictate either the national form or the definition of any particular nation. 'The generalization of commercial exchange cannot explain the creation of the modern nation; if it reveals the necessity of the unification of the so-called internal market and the elimination of obstacles to the circulation of goods and capital, *it does not in any way explain why this unification takes place precisely at the level of the nation*' (Poulantzas 1980: 105–6).

10 Perhaps the most substantial survival of such tutelage occurred in the communist world, where the Soviet Union sharply limited the actual sovereignty of East European states (not to mention constituent states of the USSR), but maintained the pretence of their autonomy. The United States arguably maintained somewhat similar relations with the Philippines and some other countries in its 'sphere of influence'. Beyond this, of course, there are questions such as whether Puerto Rico is or should be a nation-state, or should have its status within the United States 'normalized' by becoming one of the constituent states.

11 Greenfeld (1992) has analyzed the prominence of a nationalism of resentment in Central and Eastern Europe. Eley (1980, especially Chapter 5) shows this pattern vividly in the German case. Arab and Islamic nationalism have likewise been motivated by a sense of the injuries perpetrated by those with strong states (Farah 1987; Tibi 1990; Anderson *et al.* 1991; Balibar and Wallerstein 1991).

12 It is not clear whether there are objective limits on the number of viable states, as Gellner implies. If so, they clearly have not been reached.

References

Agulhon, Maurice (1981) *Marianne into Battle: Republican Imagery and Symbolism in France, 1789–1890*. Cambridge: Cambridge University Press.

Alter, Peter (1989) *Nationalism*. London: Edward Arnold.

Amin, Samir (1975) *La Crise de l'Imperialisme*. Paris: Editions de Minuit.

Anderson, Benedict (1991) *Imagined Communities*, revised edn. London: Verso (first published 1983).

Anderson, L., Khalidi, R., Muslih, M. and Simon, R. (eds) (1991) *The Origins of Arab Nationalism*. New York: Columbia University Press.

Anderson, Perry (1974) *Lineages of the Absolutist State*. London: New Left Books.

Armstrong, John A. (1982) *Nations before Nationalism*. Chapel Hill: University of North Carolina Press.

Bakken, Borge (1994) 'The exemplary society', Ph.D. thesis. Department of Sociology, University of Oslo.

Balibar, Etienne and Wallerstein, Immanuel (1991) *Race, Nation, Class*. London: Verso.

Banac, Ivo (1984) *The National Question in Yugoslavia: Origins, History, Politics*. Ithaca: Cornell University Press.

Barber, Benjamin (1995) *Jihad vs. McWorld*. New York: Times Books.

Barth, Frederick (ed.) (1969) *Ethnic Boundaries*. Oslo: Norwegian Universities Press.

Bauer, Otto ([1907]1924) *Die Nationalitätenfrage und die Sozialdemokratie*, 2nd edn, excerpted in T. Bottomore (ed.) *Austro-Marxism*. Oxford: Clarendon Press.

Beetham, David (1985) *Max Weber and the Theory of Modern Politics*, revised edn. Cambridge: Polity.

Bendix, Reinhard (1964) *Nation-Building and Citizenship*. Berkeley: University of California Press.

Benner, Erica (1995) *Really Existing Nationalisms: A Post-Communist View from Marx and Engels*. Oxford: Clarendon Press.

Berezin, Mabel (1997) *Communities of Feeling: Culture, Politics and Identity in Fascist Italy*. Ithaca: Cornell University Press.

Berezin, Mabel (forthcoming) 'Making political love: State, nation, and identity in fascist Italy', in George Steinmetz (ed.) *State/Culture*. Ithaca: Cornell University Press.

Best, Geoffrey (ed.) (1988) *The Permanent Revolution: The French Revolution and its Legacy*. Chicago: University of Chicago Press.

Billig, Michael (1995) *Banal Nationalism*. London: Sage.

Blaut, James (1987) *The National Question: Decolonizing the Theory of Nationalism*. Atlantic Highlands, NJ: Zed Books.

Bloom, William (1990) *Personal Identity, National Identity and International Relations*. Cambridge: Cambridge University Press.

Blum, Carol (1986) *Rousseau and the Republic of Virtue: The Language of Politics in the French Revolution*. Ithaca: Cornell University Press.

Bourdieu, Pierre (1976) *Outline of a Theory of Practice*. Cambridge: Cambridge University Press.

Bourdieu, Pierre (1990) *The Logic of Practice*. Stanford: Stanford University Press.

Brass, Paul (1979) 'Elite groups, symbol manipulation and ethnic identity and the Muslims of South Asia', in David Taylor and Malcolm Yapp (eds) *Political Identity in South Asia*. London: Curzon Press, pp. 85–105.

Brass, Paul (1991) *Ethnicity and Nationalism: Theory and Comparison*. New Delhi and Beverly Hills: Sage.

Brennan, Timothy (1990) 'The national longing for form', in H. Bhabha (ed.) *Nation and Narration*. London: Routledge, pp. 44–70.

Breuilly, John (1993) *Nationalism and the State*, revised edn. Chicago: University of Chicago Press (first published 1982).

Brewer, John (1989) *The Sinews of Power: War, Money and the English State, 1688–1783*. London: Unwin Hyman.

Brubaker, Rogers (1992) *Citizenship and Nationhood in France and Germany*. Cambridge, MA: Harvard University Press.

Brubaker, Rogers (1996) *Nationalism Reframed: Nationhood and the National Question in the New Europe*. Cambridge: Cambridge University Press.

Calhoun, Craig (1980) 'The authority of ancestors: A sociological reconsideration of Fortes's Tallensi in response to Fortes's critics', *Man, The Journal of the Royal Anthropological Institute*, new series, **15**, 2: 304–19.

Calhoun, Craig (1983) 'The radicalism of tradition: Community strength or venerable disguise and borrowed language?', *American Journal of Sociology*, **88**, 5: 886–914.

Calhoun, Craig (1988) 'Classical social theory and the French Revolution of 1848', *Sociological Theory*, **7**, 2: 210–25.

Calhoun, Craig (1991) 'Imagined communities and indirect relationships: Large scale social integration and the transformation of everyday life', in P. Bourdieu and J .S. Coleman (eds) *Social Theory for a Changing Society*. Boulder, CO: Westview Press, pp. 95–120.

Calhoun, Craig (1992) 'The infrastructure of modernity: Indirect relationships, information technology, and social integration', in H. Haferkamp and N. J. Smelser (eds) *Social Change and Modernity*. Berkeley: University of California Press, pp. 205–36.

Calhoun, Craig (1993a) 'New social movements of the early 19th century', *Social Science History*, **17**, 3: 385–427.

Calhoun, Craig (1993b) 'Nationalism and civil society: Democracy, diversity and self-determination', *International Sociology*, **8**, 4: 387–411.

Calhoun, Craig (1995) *Critical Social Theory: Culture, History and the Challenge of Difference*. Cambridge, MA: Blackwell.

Carr, Edward Hallett (1945) *Nationalism and After*. London: Macmillan.

Césaire, Aimée (1955) *Discourses on Nationalism*. New York: Monthly Review Press.

Chatterjee, Partha (1986) *Nationalist Thought and the Colonial World: A Derivative Discourse?* Atlantic Highlands, NJ: Zed Books.

Chatterjee, Partha (1994) *The Nation and Its Fragments: Studies in Colonial and Post-Colonial Histories*. Princeton: Princeton University Press.

Chirot, Daniel (1991) *The Crisis of Leninism and the Decline of the Left: The Revolutions of 1989*. Seattle: University of Washington Press.

Chow, Tse-tung (1960) *The May 4th Movement: Intellectual Revolution in Modern China*. Cambridge, MA: Harvard University Press.

Claudin, Fernando (1977) *The Communist Movement: From Comintern to Cominform*. Harmondsworth: Penguin.

Cohen, Jean and Arato, Andrew (1992) *The Political Theory of Civil Society*. Cambridge, MA: MIT Press.

Comaroff, John (1991) 'Humanity, ethnicity, nationality: conceptual and comparative perspectives on the USSR', *Theory and Society*, **20**: 661–87.

Connolly, William E. (1974) *The Terms of Political Discourse*. Lexington, MA: Heath.

Connor, Walker (1984) *The National Question in Marxist–Leninist Theory and Strategy*. Princeton: Princeton University Press.

Connor, Walker (1994) *Ethnonationalism*. Princeton: Princeton University Press.

Conover, Pamela and Hicks, Barbara (1996) 'The psychology of overlapping identities: Ethnic, citizen, nation, and beyond', in ARENA working paper no. 20, *Identity Formation, Citizenship and Statebuilding in the Former Communist Countries of Eastern Europe*. Oslo: ARENA.

Cushman, Thomas and Mestrovic, Stjepan G. (eds) (1996) *This Time We Knew: Western Responses to Genocide in Bosnia*. New York: New York University Press.

Davidson, Basil (1992) *Black Man's Burden: Africa and the Curse of the Nation-State*. New York: Times Books.

Debray, Regis (1977) 'Marxism and the national question', *New Left Review*, **105**, 20–41.

Delanty, Gerard (1995) *Inventing Europe*. London: Macmillan.

Denitch, Bogdan (1994) *Ethnic Nationalism: The Tragic Death of Yugoslavia*. Minneapolis: University of Minnesota Press.

Deutsch, Karl W. (1966) *Nationalism and Social Communication: An Inquiry into the Foundations of Nationality*, 2nd edn. Cambridge: MIT Press (first published 1953).

Deutsch, Karl W. (1969) *Nationalism and Its Alternatives*. New York: Knopf.

Dittkower, Frank (1993) *The Discourse of Race in Modern China*. Princeton: Princeton University Press.

Dittmer, Lowell and Kim, Samuel S. (eds) (1993) *China's Quest for National Identity*. Ithaca, NY: Cornell University Press.

Dobbs, Michael (1996) 'Milosevic, a man of the past, has dragged Serbia backward', *International Herald Tribune*, 5 August.

Donia, Robert J. and Fine, John V. A. Jr. (1994) *Bosnia and Hercegovina: A Tradition Betrayed*. London: Hurst.

Doob, Leonard (1964) *Patriotism and Nationalism: Their Psychological Foundations*. New Haven: Yale University Press.

Duara, Prasenjit (1988) *Culture, Power and the State: Rural North China, 1900–1942*. Stanford: Stanford University Press.

Duara, Prasenjit (1992) *Rescuing History from the Nation-State*. Chicago: Working Papers and Proceedings of the Center for Psychosocial Studies, no. 48.

Du Bois, W. E. B. (1989) *The Souls of Black Folk*. New York: Dover (first published 1903).

Dumont, Louis (1982) *Essays on Individualism*. Chicago: University of Chicago Press.

Durkheim, Emile (1950) *Textes*, Vol. 3 (edited by V. Karady). Paris: Editions de Minuit.

Durkheim, Emile (1984) *The Division of Labor in Society*. New York: Free Press (first published 1893).

Dyer, Gwynne (1985) *War*. New York: Crown Books.

Eisenstadt, Shmuel (1966) *Modernization, Protest and Change*. Englewood Cliffs, NJ: Prentice-Hall.

Eisenstadt, Shmuel (1973) *Building States and Nations*. Beverly Hills: Sage.

Ekeh, Peter (1990) 'Social anthropology and two contrasting uses of tribalism in Africa', *Comparative Studies in Society and History*, **32**, 4: 660–700.

Eley, Geoff (1980) *Reshaping the German Right*. Oxford: Oxford University Press.

Eley, Geoff (1992) 'Nations, publics and political cultures: Placing Habermas in the nineteenth century', in C. Calhoun (ed.) *Habermas and the Public Sphere*. Cambridge, MA: MIT Press, pp. 289–339.

Evans-Pritchard, E. E. (1940) *The Nuer*. Oxford: Oxford University Press.

Evens, Terence M. S. (1995) *Two Kinds of Rationality*. Minneapolis: University of Minnesota Press.

Fanon, Frantz (1963) *The Wretched of the Earth*. New York: Grove.

Fanon, Frantz (1965) *A Dying Colonialism*. London: Writers and Readers Press.

Farah, Tawfic E. (ed.) (1987) *Pan-Arabism and Arab Nationalism: The Continuing Debate*. Boulder: Westview Press.

Fichte, Johann Gottlieb (1968) *Addresses to the German Nation*. New York: Harper (first published 1807–8).

FitzGerald, Frances (1980) *America Revised: History School Books in the Twentieth Century*. New York: Vintage.

Fortes, Meyer (1945) *The Web of Kinship among the Tallensi of Northern Ghana*. Oxford: Oxford University Press.

Fortes, Meyer (1949) *The Dynamics of Clanship among the Tallensi of Northern Ghana*. Oxford: Oxford University Press.

Foucault, Michel (1969) *The Archaeology of Knowledge*. New York: Pantheon.

Foucault, Michel (1977) *Power/Knowledge: Selected Interviews and Other Writings, 1972–1977*. New York: Pantheon.

Foucault, Michel (1978–88) *A History of Sexuality*, Vols 1–4. New York: Pantheon.

Fraser, Nancy (1992) 'Rethinking the public sphere: A contribution to the critique of actually existing democracy', in C. Calhoun (ed.) *Habermas and the Public Sphere*. Cambridge, MA: MIT Press, pp. 109–43.

Gadamer, Hans-Georg (1975) *Truth and Method*. New York: Seabury.

Gadamer, Hans-Georg (1977) *Philosophical Hermeneutics*. Berkeley: University of California Press.

Gallie, W. B. (1967) *Philosophy and Historical Explanation*. Oxford: Oxford University Press.

Gebre-Ab, Habtu (1993) *Ethiopia and Eritrea: A Documentary Study*. Trenton: Red Sea Press.

Geertz, Clifford (1963) 'The integrative revolution: Primordial sentiments and civil politics in the new states', in C. Geertz (ed.) *Old Societies and New States: The Quest for Modernity in Asia and Africa*. New York: Free Press, pp. 107–13.

Gellner, Ernest (1964) *Thought and Change*. London: Weidenfeld and Nicolson.

Gellner, Ernest (1983) *Nations and Nationalism*. Oxford: Blackwell.

Gellner, Ernest (1995) 'Introduction', in Sukuwar Periwal (ed.) *Notions of Nationalism*. Budapest: Central European University Press.

Giddens, Anthony (1984) *The Nation State and Violence*. Berkeley: University of California Press.

Gierke, Otto Friedrich von (1934) *Natural Law and the Theory of Society*. Cambridge: Cambridge University Press.

Gilroy, Paul (1991) *Ain't No Black in the Union Jack*. Chicago: University of Chicago Press.

Gilroy, Paul (1993) *The Black Atlantic: Modernity and Double Consciousness*. Cambridge, MA: Harvard University Press.

Gladney, Dru C. (1990) 'The peoples of the People's Republic: Finally in the vanguard?', *Fletcher Forum of World Affairs*, **17**, 1: 62–76.

Godechot, Jacques (1964) *La Grande Nation*. Paris: Colin.

Greenfeld, Leah (1992) *Nationalism: Five Paths to Modernity*. Cambridge, MA: Harvard University Press.

Guibernau, Montserrat (1996) *Nationalisms: The Nation-State and Nationalism in the Twentieth Century*. Cambridge: Polity.

Haas, Ernst B. (1964) *Beyond the Nation-State: Functionalism and International Organization*. Stanford: Stanford University Press.

Habermas, Jürgen (1989) *Structural Transformation of the Public Sphere*. Cambridge, MA: MIT Press.

Habermas, Jürgen (1992) 'Citizenship and national identity: Some reflections on the future of Europe', *Praxis International*, **12**, 1: 1–19.

Habermas, Jürgen (1994) 'Struggles for recognition in the democratic constitutional state', in Amy Gutman (ed.) *Multiculturalism: Exploring the Politics of Recognition*, revised edn. Princeton: Princeton University Press.

Habermas, Jürgen (1996) *Between Facts and Norms*. Cambridge, MA: MIT Press.

Halévy, Elie (1930) *The World Crisis of 1914–1918*. Oxford: Clarendon Press.

Hall, John (1995) 'Nationalisms, classified and explained', in S. Periwal (ed.) *Notions of Nationalism*. Budapest: Central European University Press, pp. 8–33.

Hann, Chris (1995) 'Intellectuals, ethnic groups and nations: Two late-twentieth-century cases', in S. Periwal (ed.) *Notions of Nationalism*. Budapest: Central European University Press, pp. 106–28.

Hayes, Carleton J. H. (1931) *The Historical Evolution of Modern Nationalism*. New York: R. R. Smith.

Hayes, Carleton J. H. (1966) *Essays on Nationalism*. New York: Russell and Russell.

Hechter, Michael (1975) *Internal Colonialism: The Celtic Fringe in British National Development, 1536–1966*. Berkeley: University of California Press.

Hedges, Chris (1997) 'Rock singer's raucous role: Serbia's jeer leader', *New York Times*, 17 January.

Herder, Johann Gottfried (1966) *On the Origin of Language* (edited by John Moran). Chicago: University of Chicago Press.

Hintze, Otto (1975) 'Military organization and the organization of the state', in *The Historical Essays of Otto Hintze* (edited by F. Gilbert). Princeton: Princeton University Press.

Hobbes, Thomas (1976) *Leviathan*. Harmondsworth: Penguin (first published 1651).

Hobsbawm, Eric (1990) *Nations and Nationalism Since 1780: Programme, Myth, Reality*. Cambridge: Cambridge University Press.

Hobsbawm, Eric and Ranger, Terence (1983) *The Invention of Tradition*. Cambridge: Cambridge University Press.

Horowitz, David (1985) *Ethnic Groups in Conflict*. Berkeley: University of California Press.

Hoston, Germaine A. (1994) *The State, Identity, and the National Question in China and Japan*. Princeton: Princeton University Press.

Huang, Hui (1996) 'The Chinese construction of the West, 1862–1922: Discourses, actors, and the cultural field', Ph.D. dissertation. University of North Carolina at Chapel Hill.

Hunt, Lynn (1984) *Politics, Culture, and Class in the French Revolution*. Berkeley: University of California Press.

Hunt, Lynn (1992) *The Family Romance of the French Revolution*. Berkeley: University of California Press.

Hunt, Michael (1993) 'Chinese national identity and the strong state: The late Qing-Republican crisis', in Lowell Dittmer and Samuel S. Kim (eds) *China's Quest for National Identity*. Ithaca, NY: Cornell University Press, pp. 62–79.

Hutcheson, John (1994) *The Dynamics of Cultural Nationalism*, revised edn. London: Harper Collins.

Ishay, Micheline (1995) *Internationalism and its Betrayal*. Minneapolis: University of Minnesota Press.

Iyob, Ruth (1995) *The Eritrean Struggle for Independence: Domination, Resistance, Nationalism, 1941–1993*. Cambridge: Cambridge University Press.

Jalal, Ayesha (1995) 'Conjuring Pakistan: History as official imagining', *International Journal of Middle East Studies*, **27**, 1: 73–89.

Jurgensmeyer, Mark (1993) *The New Cold War? Religious Nationalism Confronts the Secular State*. Berkeley: University of California Press.

Kant, Immanuel ([1804]1970) 'Towards a perpetual peace', in H. Reiss (ed.) *Kant's Political Writings*. Cambridge: Cambridge University Press.

Keane, John (1995) 'Nations, nationalism, and European citizens', in Sukumar Periwal (ed.) *Notions of Nationalism*. Budapest: Central European University Press, pp. 182–207.

Kedourie, Elie (1994) *Nationalism*, 4th edn. Oxford: Blackwell (first published 1960).

Kennedy, Paul M. (1987) *The Rise and Fall of the Great Powers*. New York: Random House.

Kohn, Hans (1967) *The Idea of Nationalism*. New York: Collier (first published 1929).

Kohn, Hans (1968) *The Age of Nationalism*. New York: Harper and Row (first published 1944).

Kolakowski, Leszek (1992) 'Amidst moving ruins', *Daedalus* **121**, 2: 43–56.

Kramer, Lloyd (1988) *Threshold of a New World: Intellectuals and the Exile Experience in Paris, 1830–1848*. Ithaca: Cornell University Press.

Kramer, Lloyd, Reid, Donald and Barney, William (eds) (1994) *Learning History in America: Schools, Cultures, and Publics*. Minneapolis: University of Minnesota Press.

Kupchan, Charles (ed.) (1995) *Nationalism and Nationalities in the New Europe*. Ithaca: Cornell University Press.

Laitin, David (1992) *Language Repertoires and the State Construction in Africa*. Cambridge: Cambridge University Press.

Levenson, Joseph R. (1958) *Confucian China and Its Modern Fate*. Berkeley: University of California Press.

Lewis, I. M. (ed.) (1983) *Nationalism and Self-Determination in the Horn of Africa*. London: Ithaca Press.

Locke, John (1950) *Two Treatises on Government*. London: Dent (first published 1690).

McAdam, Douglas (1982) *Political Process and the Development of Black Insurgency*. Chicago: University of Chicago Press.

McAdam, Douglas (1986) 'Recruitment to high-risk activism: The case of freedom summer', *American Journal of Sociology*, **92**, 1: 64–90.

McCarthy, John and Zald, Mayer (1976) 'Resource mobilization and social movements: A partial theory', *American Journal of Sociology*, **82**, 4: 1212–41.

MacPherson, C. B. (1976) *The Political Theory of Possessive Capitalism*. Cambridge: Cambridge University Press.

Madsen, Richard (1995) *China and the American Dream*. Berkeley: University of California Press.

Malcolm, Noel (1996) *Bosnia: A Short History*, revised edn. London: Macmillan.

Mann, Michael (1986) *Sources of Social Power*, Vol. 1. Cambridge: Cambridge University Press.

Mann, Michael (1993) *Sources of Social Power*, Vol. 2. Cambridge: Cambridge University Press.

Mann, Michael (1995) 'A political theory of nationalism and its excesses', in Sukumar Periwal (ed.) *Notions of Nationalism*. Budapest: Central European University Press, pp. 44–64.

Marcu, E. D. (1976) *Sixteenth-century Nationalism*. New York: Abacus Books.

Marcus, Harold (1994) *A History of Ethiopia*. Berkeley: University of California Press.

Markakis, John (1987) *National and Class Conflict in the Horn of Africa*. Cambridge: Cambridge University Press.

Marx, Karl (1977) *Capital*, Vol. 1. Harmondsworth: Penguin (first published 1867).

Marx, Karl and Engels, Friedrich ([1848]1974) 'Manifesto of the Communist Party', in *Collected Works*, Vol. 6. London: Lawrence and Wishart, pp. 477–579.

Mauss, Marcel (1985) *Oeuvres*, Vol. 3. (edited by V. Karady). Paris: Editions de Minuit.

Mazrui, Ali and Tidy, Michael (1984) *Nationalism and New States in Africa from about 1935 to the Present*. Nairobi: Heinemann.

Meinecke, Friedrich (1970) *Cosmopolitanism and the National State*. Princeton, NJ: Princeton University.

Melikian, Souren (1997) 'Britain's imperiled heritage: Show underscores fragile state of artistic legacy', *International Herald Tribune*, 11–12 January.

Merton, Robert K. (1968) *Sociological Theory and Social Structure*, 3rd edn. Glencoe: Free Press.

Mommsen, Wolfgang (1984) *Max Weber and German Politics, 1890–1920*, revised edn. Chicago: University of Chicago Press.

Montesquieu, Charles (1976) *The Spirit of Laws*. Berkeley: University of California Press (first published 1748).

Mosse, George (1985) *Nationalism and Sexuality*. New York: Fertig.

Motyl, Alexander J. (1992) 'The modernity of nationalism: Nations, states and nation-states in the contemporary world', *Journal of International Affairs*, **45**, 3: 307–23.

Moynihan, Daniel Patrick (1993) *Pandaemonium: Ethnicity in International Politics*. Oxford: Oxford University Press.

Nadel, Siegfried (1957) *A Theory of Social Structure*. London: Cohen and West.

Nairn, Tom (1977) *The Break-Up of Britain: Crisis and Neo-Nationalism*, 2nd edn. London: New Left Books.

Nehru, Jawarhalal (1989) *The Discovery of India*. Oxford: Oxford University Press (first published 1949).

Nenarokov, Albert and Proskurin, Alexander (1983) *How the Soviet Union Solved the Nationalities Question*. Moscow: Novosti Press Agency Publishing House.

Nimni, Ephraim (1991) *Marxism and Nationalism: Theoretical Origins of a Political Crisis*. London: Pluto.

Noiriel, Gerard (1991) *La Tyrannie du National*. Paris: Calmann-Levy.

Noiriel, Gerard (1996) *The French Melting Pot*. Minneapolis: University of Minnesota Press.

Nzongola-Ntalaja (1987) 'The national question and the crisis of instability in Africa', in E. Hansen (ed.) *Africa: Perspectives on Peace and Development*. Atlantic Highlands, NJ: Zed Books, pp. 55–86.

Oberschall, Anthony (1973) *Social Conflict and Social Movements*. Englewood-Cliffs, NJ: Prentice-Hall.

Parker, Andrew, Russo, Mary, Sommer, Doris and Yaeger, Patricia (1992) *Nationalisms and Sexualities*. London: Routledge.

Pocock, J. G. A. (1975) *The Macchiavellian Moment*. Princeton: Princeton University Press.

Poggi, Gianfranco (1973) *The Rise of the State*. Stanford: Stanford University Press.

Polanyi, Karl (1944) *The Great Transformation*. Boston: Beacon.

Postone, Moishe (1993) *Time, Labour and Social Domination*. Cambridge: Cambridge University Press.

Poulantzas, Nicos (1980) *State, Power and Socialism*. London: New Left Books.

Rawls, John (1993) 'The law of peoples', in Stephen Shute and Susan Hurley (eds) *On Human Rights: The Oxford Amnesty Lectures, 1993*. New York: Basic Books.

Raychaudhuri, Tapan (1995) 'Historical reflections on the politics of Hindu communalism', *Contention*, **4**, 2: 141–62.

Renan, Ernst ([1882]1990) 'What is a nation?', in Homi Bhabha (ed.) *Nation and Narration*. London: Routledge, pp. 8–22.

Renner, Karl (1978) *The Development of the National Idea*, excerpted in T. Bottomore (ed.) *Austro-Marxism*. Oxford: Clarendon Press.

Rousseau, Jean-Jacques ([1762] 1950) 'On the social contract', in Ernest Barker (ed.) *Social Contract*. Oxford: Oxford University Press, pp. 169–307.

Rousseau, Jean-Jacques ([1771]1962) 'Considerations on the government of Poland', in *Political Writings*. Oxford: Blackwell, pp. 159–277.

Savarkar, Samagra (1937) *Wangmaya*, Vol. 6 . Poona: Maharashtra Krantik Hindu sabha (Maharashtra Revolutionary Hindu Assembly).

Schlesinger, Philip (1987) 'On national identity: Some conceptions and misconceptions criticized', *Social Science Information*, **26**, 2: 219–64.

Schlesinger, Philip (1992) '"Europeanness" – a new cultural battlefield?' *Innovation in Social Sciences Research*, **5**, 2: 1–23.

Schrecker, John (1991) *The Chinese Revolution in Historical Perspective*. New York: Praeger.

Schwarcz, Vera (1986) *The Chinese Enlightenment: Intellectuals and the*

Legacy of the May Fourth Movement of 1919. Berkeley: University of California Press.

Schwartz, Benjamin (1964) *In Search of Wealth and Power: Yen Fu and the West.* Cambridge, MA: Harvard University Press.

Schwarzmantel, John (1991) *Socialism and the Idea of the Nation.* Hemel Hempstead: Harvester Wheatsheaf.

Selassie, Bereket Habte (1980) *Conflict and Intervention in the Horn of Africa.* London: Gordon and Breech.

Selassie, Bereket Habte (1989) *Eritrea and the United Nations.* Trenton: Red Sea Press.

Seton-Watson, Hugh (1977) *Nations and States.* Boulder, CO: Westview.

Sheehan, James J. (1978) *German Liberalism in the Nineteenth Century.* Chicago: University of Chicago Press.

Shils, Edward (1957) 'Primordial, personal, sacred and civil ties', *British Journal of Sociology*, **8**, 2: 130–45.

Shils, Edward (1981) *Tradition.* Chicago: University of Chicago Press.

Skocpol, Theda (1979) *States and Social Revolutions.* Cambridge: Cambridge University Press.

Skurnowicz, Joan S. (1981) *Romantic Nationalism and Liberalism: Joachim Lelewel and the Polish National Idea.* New York: Columbia University Press.

Smith, Anthony (1973) 'Nationalism', *Current Sociology*, **21**: 7–128.

Smith, Anthony (1983) *Theories of Nationalism.* London: Duckworth.

Smith, Anthony (1986) *The Ethnic Origins of Nations.* Oxford: Blackwell.

Smith, Anthony (1991) *National Identity.* London: Penguin.

Snyder, Louis (1982) *Global Mini-Nationalisms: Autonomy or Independence?* Westport, CT: Greenwood.

Snyder, Louis (1984) *Macro-Nationalisms: A History of the Pan-Movements.* Westport, CT: Greenwood.

Spence, Jonathan (1990) *The Search for Modern China.* New York: Norton.

Spencer, Herbert ([1853]1974) *The Evolution of Society: Selections from Herbert Spencer's 'Principles of Sociology',* (edited by Robert L. Carneiro). Chicago: University of Chicago Press.

Stalin, Josef (1976) *Marxism and the National and Colonial Question.* New York: International Publishers (first published 1914).

Steiner, George (1988) 'Aspects of counter-revolution', in P. Best (ed.) *The French Revolution.* Chicago: University of Chicago Press, pp. 129–55.

Sutton, M. (1982) *Nationalism, Positivism and Catholicism: The Politics of Charles Maurras and French Catholics 1890–1914.* Cambridge: Cambridge University Press.

Szporluk, Roman (1988) *Communism and Nationalism: Karl Marx vs. Friedrich List.* New York: Oxford University Press.

Tamir, Yael (1993) *Liberal Nationalism.* Princeton: Princeton University Press.

Taylor, Charles (1990) *Sources of the Self*. Cambridge, MA: Harvard University Press.

Thomas, George and Meyer, John (1984) 'The expansion of the state', *Annual Review of Sociology*, 10: 461–82.

Thrower, Norman J.W. (1996) *Maps and Civilization: Cartography in Culture and Society*. Chicago: University of Chicago Press.

Tibi, Bassam (1990) *Arab Nationalism: A Critical Enquiry*, 2nd edn. Translated by M. F. Sluglett and Peter Sluglett. New York: Saint Martin's Press.

Tilly, Charles (ed.) (1975) *The Formation of National States in Western Europe*. Princeton: Princeton University Press.

Tilly, Charles (1978) *From Mobilization to Revolution*. Reading, MA: Addison-Wesley.

Tilly, Charles (1984) *Big Questions, Large Processes, Huge Comparisons*. New York: Russell Sage Foundation.

Tilly, Charles (1990) *Coercion, Capital and European States, AD 990–1990*. Cambridge: Blackwell.

Tiryakian, Edward and Rogowski, Donald (eds) (1985) *New Nationalisms in the Developed West*. Boston: Allen and Unwin.

Todorov, Istvan (1990) *Nous et les autres*. Paris: Editions de Seuill.

Trevor-Roper, Hugh (1983) 'The invention of tradition: The highland tradition of Scotland', in E. Hobsbawm and T. Ranger (eds) *The Invention of Tradition*. Cambridge: Cambridge University Press, pp. 15–42.

Ullmann, Walter (1977) *Political Theories of the Middle Ages*. Harmondsworth: Penguin.

van der Veer, Peter (1994) *Religious Nationalism: Hindus and Muslims in India*. Berkeley: University of California Press.

Wallerstein, Immanuel (1974–88) *The Modern World System*, Vols 1–3. La Jolla: Academic Press.

Walzer, Michael (1983) *Spheres of Justice*. New York: Free Press.

Walzer, Michael (1992) *Just and Unjust Wars*, 2nd edn. New York: Basic Books.

Warnke, Georgia (1987) *Gadamer: Hermeneutics, Tradition and Reason*. Stanford, CA: Stanford University Press.

Watkins, Susan Cott (1992) *Provinces into Nations: Demographic Diversity in Europe, 1880–1960*. Princeton: Princeton University Press.

Weber, Eugen (1976) *Peasants into Frenchmen*. Stanford: Stanford University Press.

Weber, Marianne (1988) *Max Weber: An Intellectual Biography*. New Brunswick: Transaction.

Weber, Max (1976) *Economy and Society*. Berkeley: University of California Press (first published 1922).

Weintraub, Jeff (1997) 'Introduction', in Jeff Weintraub and Krishan

Kumar (eds) *Public and Private in Thought and Practice*. Chicago: University of Chicago Press.

White, Harrison (1992) *Identity and Control*. Princeton: Princeton University Press.

Wittgenstein, Ludwig (1953) *Philosophical Investigations*. Oxford: Blackwell.

Zacek, Joseph F. (1969) 'Nationalism in Czechoslovakia', in Peter F. Sugar and Ivo J. Lederer (eds) *Nationalism in Eastern Europe*. Seattle: University of Washington Press.

Zaret, David (1996) 'Petitions and the "Invention" of public opinion in the English revolution', *American Journal of Sociology*, **101**, 6: 1497–555.

Index